Journeys of Discovery

TRANSITIONS, RITES OF PASSAGE, AND THE SACRAMENTAL LIFE OF FAITH

Fr. Wilson,

May God bless you and your loved ones with hope, health, and happiness!

Peace,

Fr. Bob Hater
Dallas Ministry Conference
October 23, 2009

Journeys of Discovery

Transitions, Rites of Passage, and the Sacramental Life of Faith

ROBERT J. HATER, PhD

Dedication

This book is dedicated to
my parents, Stanley and Olivia Hater,
whose inspiration and faith
guided me through many life transitions

It is also dedicated to
my brother-in-law, James D. Kohl,
whose commitment to his family and the Catholic faith
inspired others to live a better life.
On Christmas Eve, December 24, 2006,
right after dinner, as he prepared to distribute
Christmas gifts to his family, he died suddenly.

May they rest in peace!

Acknowledgments

In preparing this book manuscript, I received valuable feedback from Sr. Jeanette Jabour, O.P., Mary Riportella, Carol Smith, Thomas Stark, and Rosanne Thomas. They read it critically and offered insightful comments. I am grateful and express my appreciation for the time and effort they expended to make this a better book. I also thank Gina Meyer, the pastoral minister cited anonymously, and the family of James Kohl for giving me permission to use the materials cited in this book.

I also acknowledge the use of the following books in preparing this work.

Allport, Gordon W. *The Individual and His Religion*.

Fourez, Gerard. *Sacraments and Passages*. Notre Dame, IN: Ave Maria Press, 1983.

Hater, Robert J. *When a Catholic Marries a Non-Catholic*. Cincinnati: St. Anthony Messenger Press, 2006.

Ludwig, Theodore M. *The Sacred Paths*. New York: Macmillan Publishing Company, 1989.

Van Der Leeuw, G. *Religion in Essence and Manifestation, vol. 1*. New York: Harper and Row, 1963.

Van Gennep, Arnold. *Rites of Passage*. Trans. M. Vizedom and G. Caffee. Chicago: University of Chicago Press, 1960.

Winseman, Albert, et. al. *Living Your Strengths*. Catholic Edition. New York: Gallup Press, 2006.

TWENTY-THIRD PUBLICATIONS
A Division of Bayard
One Montauk Avenue, Suite 200
New London, CT 06320
(860) 437-3012 or (800) 321-0411
www.23rdpublications.com

ISBN 978-1-58595-708-8
Library of Congress Catalog Card Number: 2008933182

Printed in the U.S.A.

Contents

Introduction

These days, when the traditional ties that hold family members in a tight-knit unit are loosening, churches are searching for ways to help their members grow spiritually and to respond to Jesus' message. Traditional commitments to ancestral faith have waned. At one time, family members professed the same beliefs and worshipped at the same church. Contact with other faith traditions was minimal. When I was a child, only one Protestant woman lived on our street. Today, many of my friends and associates profess other beliefs. We live in ecumenical environments, take trips around the world, work in multi-ethnic settings, and marry people of other faiths.

Society has become much more complex. We travel more extensively and the earth becomes smaller. We can go almost anywhere in the United States in five hours. Materialistic lifestyles and social pressures demand more money and increase pressures on our time and relationships. As this happens, traditional customs and stable life patterns slip away. The past presumption that Christians attend their own churches each Sunday has disappeared. Today, a "cafeteria" mentality may move many to abandon traditional churches and seek those that fulfill their immediate needs.

Parish leaders and ministers address the needs of busy, secular-minded people looking for hope and deeper roots. Parishes are responding in multiple ways. Ministry often takes the form of new programs and activities, employing modern communication techniques and graphics to present Christ's message through mass media. While using the insights of social scientists and media experts has value, however, it results in only limited success. Something is missing.

Trying to find the right program to use may not be the best approach. In this pastoral book we address, instead, deep human needs by *ministering to people at key times*, when they seek a deeper message and are more open to the wisdom that Christ and his church can offer.

This book invites parish ministers to address such key times—described simply as *transition times* or *life transitions*—because they are great opportunities to present the message of Jesus and the church. During such transition times, people look for insight and support. Pastoral ministers can use life's transitions to help people to grow in faith.

Part One sets the stage.

- Chapter One considers transition times, rites of passage, culture, and history. It indicates how world cultures and religions use rites of passage to address life's mysteries.
- Chapter Two considers community and personal perspectives.
- Chapter Three looks at life changes as they happen in a linear and/or cyclic perspective in open or closed societies. This chapter examines insights gleaned from each approach that suggest profound implications for today.
- Chapter Four addresses transition times in relation to human experience, faith, and Jesus. Each chapter offers Jesus and Mary as our models, reflections on faith formation, and suggestions for reflection and action.

Part Two looks at life experiences as opportunities for growth in faith.

- Chapter Five considers beginnings in life.
- Chapter Six treats life changes and growth.
- Chapter Seven considers joys, celebrations, and accomplishments.
- Chapter Eight reflects on life tragedies, and
- Chapter Nine discusses endings and new beginnings. Each chapter considers a key transition time, like birth.

The chapters are divided into four parts. Each one

- considers what the chapter will cover
- tells a story and examines a transition time, analyzes it in light of Jesus and Mary as our models, and considers its importance for faith formation
- reviews the key points learned
- offers discussion questions based on the chapter.

The book is written for pastoral ministers and the general reader. It avoids language that would be unclear to the average adult.

PART ONE
Setting the Stage

This introduction to Part One sets the stage for subsequent chapters. After beginning with a story from my personal experience with my father, it indicates that

- stories tell the human story and thus touch all of our lives,
- they connect with Jesus' story, and
- they reflect fundamental life patterns.

This part stresses the importance of acknowledging and responding to such universal human patterns.

After a conference in San Diego, California, a woman told me, "You did not tell your stories, you told mine." During my address, I described my father's prolonged sickness, including his last Holy Saturday on earth with Mom and me. After his death, I wrote the following reflection.

> On the day before Easter, Mom and I wanted to get Dad a nice gift. We asked him what he wanted. He said, "Nothing, I don't need anything. I'll never swing another hammer or drive my car again. I need nothing material. The only thing I need is your love. You are my gifts this Easter."
>
> Still wanting to buy him something, Mom and I went to the store. We looked to no avail. Finally, we smiled at each other. Mom said, "Stanley is right. He needs nothing, we ARE his Easter gifts." To symbolize our love, we bought him a yellow flower and put it on our living room table. This was especially appropriate, for Dad loved to work in the yard. His favorite

> pastime was taking care of his flowers. When he saw the flower, he smiled. It reminded him of our love and God's love, celebrated on the next day.
>
> On Easter Sunday, we gathered around the table. The flower spoke of our love for Dad and his love for us. It symbolized also the love of God and of Jesus' love, which makes our love possible.

Why did the woman at the conference say that my stories were her stories? The major reason was that recently, her father had died. My story spoke to her great love for her own father. By using Jesus' story to connect with my story, she clarified how God was with her during her dad's last days.

Deep stories always connect with people, for they tell the human story, not the story of one person alone. Such stories include joy and sorrow, humor and pathos. They draw the listener into a dimension that goes beyond the present reality to a spiritual realm where the Spirit dwells and healing happens. Deep stories connect with fundamental questions that all people share because they are human.

These human stories connect with Jesus' story. To discover ultimate wisdom in our stories, we probe into God's wisdom found in Scripture, especially in Jesus' words. We are more open to discovering this wisdom when we are vulnerable, those times when we experience our humanity more clearly. This occurs at important life transitions, like birth and death.

Deep stories reflect fundamental life patterns that are common to all people. These include life and death, growth, suffering, joy, and celebration. They have been present ever since God created the human race. This section stresses the importance of acknowledging and responding to such universal human patterns.

Part One sets the stage for what follows in Part Two. It considers transition times as special opportunities for faith formation. At key life moments we are invited to open ourselves to the Holy Spirit, who helps us grow in knowledge and wisdom. Let's begin.

CHAPTER ONE

Life's Transitions, Rites of Passage, and Culture

This chapter sets the stage for a deeper analysis of key transition times and rites of passage. We begin taking a deeper look by

- → telling the story of the old tree;
- → examining transition times and their relation to rites of passage. We consider fundamental attitudes and rituals, culture as a delivery system, changing cultural contexts, and stories and basic beliefs;
- → considering Jesus and Mary as our models;
- → seeing transition times as opportunities for faith formation.

Next, we review the main points of this chapter. Finally, we offer some discussion questions.

Take a Deeper Look

> Broken, rotted branches lie at the foot of the once proud apple tree standing in the backyard. Thirty-five years ago, Stanley and Olivia Hater, my parents, bought this small twig of a tree at the local nursery and waited patiently for it to mature. Year after year, it grew and produced luscious apples to feed the family.
>
> Several years ago, a large deer, attempting to get some of the lower branch apples, broke off a major limb. From that time on, the tree began a profound struggle for life. After a while termites took over the bottom of the tree, but the apples still came, as the tree gradually died.
>
> Year after year, more dead branches fell off, and limb after limb turned brown and rotted. Eventually, the chain saw did its job on the dead branches until only one large limb made its way heavenward. This year, surprisingly, beautiful buds appeared on the remaining branches and, as the summer wore on, the apples grew to one inch in diameter. Then, just as mysteriously as apples appeared from the blossoms, they shriveled up and died. No matter how the tree tried, its deteriorating condition prohibited the apples from coming to maturity. Soon, the tree will die completely, following the universal law that there is a time for everything—a time to be born and a time to die.

The story of the tree is repeated by every creature that ever lived on this earth—plants, animals, and humans. All are engulfed by the cycle of birth and death. Everything is in transition, nothing stands still. There is morning and evening, sunrise and sunset, joy and sorrow, birth and death.

As pastoral ministers, family members, and friends, we are invited to take the wisdom gleaned from reflecting on the story of the old apple tree to ask how it can inspire us to minister more effectively. As we know, all people experience life tragedies and all go through hard times. The same tensions symbolized by the dying tree, and the eventual deaths of Stanley and Olivia, affect every person who loses a loved one, is beset with a serious sickness, loses a child through a miscarriage, or suffers other kinds of loss. As parish ministers we experience such events every day.

It's easy, over time, to become immune to the sufferings that people experience when such things happen. This can never become the norm in parish ministry. If it does, we lose one of the most effective means of evangelization open to us. Take the following episode.

> The parish ministers at St. Mark's parish experienced tension among themselves. Several left, others had difficulty communicating with each other, and still others were not well. And yet, the needs of parish members did not end.
>
> One morning the secretary received word that a man died and his family wished to have a Catholic funeral Mass. No one knew the family. The staff discussed the situation. The bereavement minister said that he was going out of town, so would not be available. The pastor planned to celebrate the Mass and funeral rites, but to do little more himself to minister to the family after the service.
>
> One parish minister, Esther, was not comfortable with the plan. After work, she spoke to several parish friends. Next, Esther contacted the family, helped them with arrangements, and planned a reception at the parish afterwards. Her friends prepared food and drinks.

During the reception, the deceased man's son thanked Esther profusely. He said, "You'll never know how your kindness affected our family. We are very grateful." Who knows how many family members and friends returned to the church because of Esther's kindness!

The grieving family experienced a significant transition in their lives with the death of their father. The funeral Mass and reception marked an important rite of passage that helped them move toward eventual healing.

Life's transitions are times that change our life focus.

Throughout history, people have developed rituals to address such life transitions as birth, adolescence, marriage, sickness, retirement, and death. We call these rituals *rites of passage*. Considering them from a historical, communal, or personal perspective, however, is incomplete. We must see them within the larger perspective of life.

We are earth creatures, subject to the dynamics present in life itself. This was evident in the lives of Stanley and Olivia, who planted the apple tree. They gave it special care—watering, feeding, and pruning it. They grew old with the apple tree. Eventually, Stanley died and the apple tree lived on. For many years, Olivia cared for the tree, picked its fruit, and froze the apples for pies. She and the tree aged together and a special bond joined them. Shortly after Olivia died, the tree ceased producing fruit and deteriorated rapidly. Eventually, the tree also died.

The tree story shows that all life can serve as a meditation on our personal lives. The transitions occurring in nature remind us that we change at key life moments. As humans, we can know these changes, face them, and become better persons. Such transition times are opportunities for new and deeper kinds of awareness and growth.

Each transition invites us to probe life's mysteries and see how God penetrates life's veil to disclose new insights into who we are and why we are here. These are wonderful opportunities for us to reach out to joyful or suffering friends and neighbors, urging them to walk with hope on their unique life path.

Transition Times and Rites of Passage

Important life transitions, like birth, marriage, sickness, healing, death, and burial, are more than *mere events*. They are *transition times in life* and need to be ritualized by rites of passage which connect them to a deeper source of energy or power (G. Van Deer Leeuw, *Religion in Essence and Manifestation*, 1963, pp. 192-93). Consider, for example, the following parish episode.

> A rite of passage is a ritual enacted by a group to mark the passage of one or more people through a significant life cycle.
>
> Arnold Van Gennup, **Rites of Passage**, 1960

> Sean and Kim were nearly forty and wanted to have a child. Finally, after years of waiting, Kim became pregnant. It became an event for the parish leaders, for Sean ministered at Nativity parish as the music director. He and his wife were actively involved in several ministries in this wonderful, faith-filled community.
>
> As the months passed, Kim began to have problems and was bedridden during the final month before giving birth. When the anticipated day came, the doctor informed them that the child was stillborn.

> The couple was devastated. So were their families and friends. Parish ministers wondered how to help them cope. It was decided with their approval to have a prayer service at their home and invite family and close parish members. The funeral Mass was to follow a week later.
>
> At the prayer service, the couple had the opportunity to cry and celebrate with those they loved in the intimate surroundings of their home. Sean and Kim helped prepare the celebration of their child's entrance into eternal life that day and during the funeral Mass in the parish church the following week.

After these two celebrations, Sean told me that, "The double celebration helped us see that grieving is not a once for all event. It doesn't end with the celebration of a Mass. After the funeral Mass, most participants go off to their homes and workplaces, often forgetting that those who grieve are just beginning to experience the implications of their loss. The fact that our two celebrations were a week apart helped us begin the grieving process with a rite of passage in faith and continue it ritualistically at the funeral Mass."

Kim reiterated Sean's comments and wondered what it might have been like if they hadn't celebrated with rites of passage at this traumatic time in their married life. As she said, "During this period, the support of the community, the prayers of the church, and our faith enabled us to experience a deeper healing power of God than any of us could have imagined possible."

It is not sufficient to experience transition times and recall them later. They must be *ritualized* or *celebrated* to recognize their full significance:

- Parents experience a child's coming into the world and ritualize this event with gifts, cards, and parties.
- Christians have a baby baptized.

- People recognize the significance of marriage or graduation by experiencing the event and celebrating it.

Any significant transitional time, considered merely as an event without ritualizing it through a rite of passage, is empty and incomplete. This consideration contains three important notions.

1. A difference exists between the actual *transition time, happening, or event* (birth or death), and its *ritualization or celebration through a rite of passage* (baptism or a funeral rite).
2. A deep connection exists between the rite of passage (ritualizing a person's going into the military or getting married) and a deeper source of energy. For ancient people the rite of passage helped connect the one experiencing it with an ultimate giver of energy (Van Der Leeuw, p. 27). In Christianity this is God. A rite of passage invites one into contact with this source of energy or power (the Trinity in Baptism) or gives an additional increase or loss of power (job loss or promotion). The energy or power is connected with God, not as the one who *directly* gives or takes it away (health and sickness), but as its *ultimate* source.
3. Rites of passage are always *transitional or passing* and involve a degree of uncertainty and vulnerability. Because of their transitory nature they point to an unchanging source, namely God.

We gain added insights into such transitional times from other cultures. The Chinese celebrate a custom known as *passing through the gate* repeatedly in a child's early life (Van Der Leeuw, p. 193). It may occur yearly, less frequently, or when a child is sick. Those involved pass ceremoniously through a bamboo gate, a symbol of life. The child's birth is not considered a *definitive event*, if no one celebrates or ritualizes it (Van Der Leeuw, p. 193).

The wisdom gleaned from such rituals tells us that celebrating events like birth, marriage, or other transition times through rites of passage completes them by taking them beyond mere events and joining them to a deeper source of sacred power coming from God and mediated by a community. For instance, Christian rites of passage, like baptism or the Eucharist, which celebrate membership in Christ's Body, are imbued with saving graces gained by Jesus on the cross.

The relationship between the *event* and its *celebration* helps us appreciate why it hurts if no one wishes us a happy birthday. This recognition helped the Dorswick children see why their mother was very happy when they gave her a surprise seventy-fifth birthday party.

Rites of passage are important moments for the community and the individual. They provide opportunities to increase or lessen responsibilities in a group (becoming a head nurse, returning to the classroom to teach, or retiring). At each significant life change, one's energies and responsibilities shift focus. Ritualizing transitional times helps people begin or move on.

Rites of passage require ritual separation from a former life, acknowledgment of a profound happening, and integration into the next stage in community life (Theodore M. Ludwig, *The Sacred Paths*, p. 65, and Gerard Fourez, *Sacraments and Passages*).

Celebrating rites of passage helps a person separate from an old lifestyle and move into a new one (single to married, married to divorced). In this context, Margo, a divorced woman said, "Unlike the death of a spouse, the end of a marriage is largely ignored by the community."

Since changing times afford new responsibilities, opportunities, and a closer connection with God, efforts must be made to relate to others according to the new state of life, not shy away from them or become isolated. Community rituals and celebrations help people make important life transitions. Help from the wider community is essential.

Rites of passage intensify the tensions that exist through life. No language adequately expresses the built-in tensions that accompany difficult times. While words often are inadequate, rituals have real value, as indicated in the following episode.

> When Stephanie, the mother of seven children, became seriously ill and was unable to speak, her husband and children kept constant vigil by her bedside. Visitors entering the room were struck by the love they shared with her. They held her hands, rubbed her forehead, and kissed her cheek. Their words expressed their love, but they did not say as much as their physical expressions of love. Their constant ritual of affection said more than their words conveyed.

Ritual manifestations, like holding a sick person's hand or giving a hug to a hurting person, connect with the tensions experienced by sick or grieving parties. Often, such actions address tensions more adequately than words. In sickness and death, words of regret may ring hollow, whereas sensitive actions may connect with the tension involved (Fourez, *Sacraments and Passages*).

A historical context can shed further light on the *event* and its *celebration* in rites of passage. When introducing a graduate course on Symbol and Myth, one professor, Dr. Robsmith, begins with early civilizations. Students learn from cave paintings, artifacts, and ancient records that rituals are universal. They also discuss rites of passage still practiced by some native tribes.

One ancient rite of passage formerly used by an African tribe initiated adolescent boys into adulthood. Adult males took the boys into the bush, painted them white, and put them in coffin-like boxes, symbolizing death to childhood and birth to manhood. The rite included screams and sounds, intended eventually to dispel fear and allow the boys to face manhood with courage. Sometimes this rite lasted for weeks, as they fasted, eating only what was necessary to maintain their health.

The girl's initiation rites were different. They usually began at their first menstrual period and lasted until the birth of the first child. A wise woman of the tribe mentored each girl, who remained in her family home. The emphasis in the boy's and girl's rites was on life—protecting tribal life in the case of the boys, and giving new life in the case of the girls.

After a class on rites of passage, Joe, an African American student in his early forties, told Dr. Robsmith,

> Forgive me for smiling, but while I listened to you speak about African rites of passage, I heard something similar to what I experienced as an adolescent. Your descriptions reminded me of my experience. I was initiated into manhood through our tribe's adolescent rites in the African jungle.
>
> Soon after my initiation at fourteen, missionaries evangelized our village and our family converted to Christianity. I attended the mission school. There, I got a good education and eventually made my way to the United States. I will always be an African and intend one day to return to my village to care for my elderly father.

After Joe described his initiation rite, Dr. Robsmith better appreciated the power of such an event for the individual and the tribe. The lessons that Joe learned underlie his basic attitudes, even though he is now Christian and half a world away from his homeland.

We can learn from Joe the critical role that rites of passage play in culture, community, and personal life. This appreciation helps us see the challenges presented by Western societies, where rites of passage have nearly disappeared or become secularized in the form of personal fulfillment in sex, money, and achievement. Joe's story also challenges pastoral ministers to investigate ways they can celebrate key moments in the lives of their parishioners.

Fundamental Attitudes and Rituals

Why are rites of passage significant? Rooted in life, the endless cycle of coming and going, birth and death, success and failure are part of nature's laws. They touch life's creative energies.

To walk in harmony with life, we must move with the rhythms established by God for nature's good ordering. The ordering of nature requires us to live according to creation's laws. Plant, animal, and human harmony and the endless cycle of birth and death manifest these laws. From them, we learn fundamental attitudes concerning life, which root the dynamics inherent in every culture. Thus, for instance, the orientation of a child brought up in a religious environment (Jewish, Muslim, or Christian) differs from that of a child raised with no religious upbringing. United States citizens develop different attitudes from people in other cultures (e.g., Kenya, Borneo, or Japan). People in every culture learn ways of ritualizing their beliefs.

> Rituals are regular and patterned rhythms or ways of acting that give life direction and purpose.

Ritual patterns are vital to human survival. We see them in seasons of the year, plant life, and animal migration patterns. We see them in human celebrations of birth, marriage, old age, and religious rituals.

Human rituals manifest basic attitudes and beliefs. Consider the priority that various cultures put on family life. Some non-Western people living in the United States remark how their commitments to family are deeper than that of their American neighbors, who may go weeks without speaking to or eating with family members.

Contemporary secular rituals that stress money and affluence reflect functional values. When society secularizes core values, the concurrent rituals and life passages are secularized as well. This happens when we root happiness in material things rather than in love and sacrifice.

A contrast exists between attitudes toward the elderly in Western and non-Western cultures. The latter cultures respect the wisdom of older people. They seek their advice and encourage them to teach children about life's values. This is clearly perceived in the following ancient African custom:

> When a boy is old enough, his grandfather takes him into the forest outside of the village. Together they select a small tree for the grandson and plant it at the edge of the village. It is the child's responsibility to care for it. As the child grows, the grandfather sits with him under the old man's special tree. In its shade, he teaches the boy the secrets of life and recounts tribal stories. Here, the boy learns the values that really count, especially commitment to God, family, and tribe. The boy internalizes the meaning of these stories as he grows and cares for his own tree.
>
> When the boy's tree is mature, he has become a man. Eventually, his grandfather dies, the boy marries, has a family, and one day becomes a grandfather. In turn, he takes his grandson to the forest, selects a tree for the boy, and plants it. Like his grandfather before him, he now sits under his own tree, planted in childhood, and teaches his grandson the mysteries of life that his grandfather taught him. The cycle goes on, as each generation learns life's wisdom from the elders, sitting under their tree.

This custom reflects the tribe's respect for elder members. It provides a good sense of a civilization's direction from its ritual patterns with older people. Contrasted with African rites of passage, some retirement homes reflect our own culture's disjointed values.

Culture as Delivery System

Cultures are delivery systems for core truths people believe. Outsiders do not always understand a culture's core message, because they do not understand the cultural values depicted or the rituals celebrated. An example of this occurred during a conference of Mexican people in a United States border town.

> Over five hundred attended a session on Christian mission and ministry. The formal education of most participants stopped early in life, when they went to work in the fields. They attended the conference, eager to learn about their Catholic faith and how it related to life.
>
> After the speaker concluded, an elderly man approached the stage and spoke to the presenter saying, "You did not give us United States theology. You spoke Mexican theology because you told stories. That's the way we do theology." Stories reflect core truths in his culture.
>
> Mexican culture was evident also in an episode that baffled the speaker. During intermission, many women hurriedly left the room. The woman facilitator asked the speaker if he noticed them and what he thought of the exodus. The speaker answered, "I assume they left to attend to their physical needs or other commitments." She said, "This is not the reason. To understand their action, you must appreciate their culture. The women are close to their families.

> At the break, they hurried to the phone to call their families to make sure everything was okay at home and to inform them that they were fine."
>
> Then the facilitator asked the speaker if he noticed the seventy-five people in the back of the auditorium who talked during his address. He said, "Yes," but said they were not a distraction. She apologized for not telling him beforehand that catechists were with them, translating his words for those who did not understand English.

The lesson of this episode applies to other cultures. People see life's meaning in light of their cultural norms. What they develop may be hard for others to appreciate. Some of their conclusions may be questionable, but they make sense to them. Today's teenage culture often reflects a similar dynamic. While adults admire their zeal, energy, and positive contributions, they may not always appreciate a teenager's music, dress, and lifestyle. Most adolescents offer hope for the future, even though some are misguided. Whatever their stance toward life, it usually makes sense to them.

Culture's impact applies to a juvenile gang or a religious group's activities. Gang initiations and various initiation rites indicate in different ways the importance of rites of passage in the cultures that practice them. This applies also to different approaches to freedom in Western and Muslim cultures. The inability to appreciate values present in another culture blocks the communication of core values.

Changing Cultural Context

Rites of passage celebrating core issues connect with universal human patterns. Such rites exist, irrespective of the culture. Cultures address birth and death differently. Early Jewish history does not reveal belief in personal immortality. Hence, Hebrew rites of passage at death did not focus on personal survival in the afterlife, but concentrated on living on through descendants. By the time of the Maccabees, two hundred years before Christ, belief in personal existence in an afterlife began to take hold. When Jesus lived, the Pharisees held this belief, while the Sadducees denied it. Their beliefs affected their rites of passage dealing with death. Christians ritualize their beliefs differently from their Jewish ancestors in faith.

When cultural beliefs shift, rites of passage also change.

A recent example of change in cultural beliefs, with implications for rites of passage, can be seen the case of marriage and divorce in our country. Not long ago, marriage was the norm and divorce was rare (some states even outlawed it except in rare instances). "No fault" divorce didn't exist. Today, marriage does not have the same definitive character, largely due to a significant rise in the rate of divorce. Marriage and divorce have taken on a different focus, calling for new ways to ritualize the movement from married to single life.

Pastoral ministers need to remember that some Catholics believe they cannot receive Communion after divorce. Sometimes, for this and other reasons, divorced Catholics drift away from the church. To help them at this difficult time, pastoral ministers need to consider setting up prayerful, pastoral sessions for the divorced. This can include rites of passage, celebrated in faith, to assist the divorced person in his or her continued journey with God and the Catholic community.

Society's regard for women has changed as well. Before the feminist movement, most girls worked for a while after graduating from high school and then got married. When these women married and began having children, most quit their jobs and worked in the home. This was their normal passage into adulthood. Today, as we all know, many women graduate from college, begin a career, and then marry. Often, they remain in the workforce even after children come.

Religious rites of passage can shift focus also. Formerly, many Catholic parents believed infants who died before baptism never entered heaven to see God. Consequently, they had their children baptized shortly after birth. Many Catholics no longer hold this belief. They put off baptism for months or years. Something similar has occurred with Mass attendance. In my childhood, we were taught that it was a mortal sin to miss Mass on Sunday without a good reason. Mass was the center of a Catholic's Sunday. Today, many Catholics do not go to Mass weekly.

Rites of passage, once centering on spiritual realties, sometimes assume a secular focus. Parents, grandparents, and family members with deep faith celebrate baptism as a baby's entrance into the new life of Christ. Others, not steeped in faith, regard it as a family, rather than a faith, event. For them, it has lost its spiritual meaning, significance, and power.

Stories and Basic Beliefs

The Kateri Native Conference of Canada invited Jim, a parish minister, to give several sessions at their pastoral gathering in Thunder Bay, Ontario. As the time approached, he sought more information about their expectations. The elder who invited Jim said. "Just tell stories." Since the conference centered on family life, he planned to tell family stories but did not know how to arrange them. His cultural background was not the same as theirs. He asked the elder, "Should I begin with my stories? "No," she replied. "We will begin with *our* stories, and then you tell your stories."

As the conference began, Jim learned that his stories connected with theirs. Hearing their stories and listening to his was never a problem, for, like him, they place high priority on celebrating family and community stories through rites of passage. This conference provided Jim a firsthand understanding of how native peoples ritualize fundamental beliefs through rites of passage. Past evidence of this is found in

- cave paintings, Egyptian tombs, and sacred Hindu books;
- Chinese art testifying to the need to celebrate life experiences, such as birth or marriage;
- native episodes depicting enemy conquest, spring planting, and fall harvest;
- Hebrew and Christian historical records reinforce the same experiences, as do rituals around the world.

Through the ages people's stories and rituals probed into nature's mysteries. The cultures they describe vary, but the patterns underlying them are the same, for all deep stories go beyond cultural expression. As we consider the way culture ritualizes fundamental beliefs, we learn more by reflecting on major events in Jesus' life. In so doing, his response can become a model for us to follow.

Jesus as Model

For Jesus and faithful Jews of his time, the Jewish culture served as a delivery system that taught them about God's covenant with the Chosen People. Here, they learned the basic beliefs and practices of their faith. Jesus observed his Jewish faith faithfully. He followed the teachings of the Law and prophets. He was taught by Mary and Joseph to be a good Jewish boy and to attend the synagogue. There he learned the Torah and underwent the rites of passage prescribed in the Law.

Mary, his mother, must have been very proud when Jesus was circumcised shortly after his birth and then was brought to the Temple for purification as required by the Law of Moses (Luke 2:22). He continued his fidelity to the Law at his Bar Mitzvah and regular synagogue attendance and learned the Jewish ways by his fidelity to Jewish beliefs and practices.

Within the Jewish society, such rituals initiated him into life. As an adult, Jesus challenged the Scribes and Pharisees, not because he questioned the tenets of Judaism, but because their teaching sometimes deviated from the authentic interpretation of the Law. He pointed out how the teachings of the Scribes and Pharisees strayed from God's Law when his disciples ate the leftover grain from the field and he cured a man with a paralyzed hand on the Sabbath (Luke 6:1–5 and Luke 6:6–10).

When Jesus prepared for the Last Supper, he observed the Jewish precepts concerning Passover. The long-standing traditions of his forefathers remained intact as he celebrated this rite of passage with his friends and disciples. During the meal, Jesus took bread and wine, blessed them, changed them into his body and blood, and gave them to his disciples. This is the food of the new Covenant, making present for all time his flesh and blood poured out for humankind on the cross. At the Last Supper, Jesus gave us the *Eucharist*, the great sacrament of thanksgiving.

This simple act initiated a profound change in the way that his followers celebrated Passover, the great memorial of Judaism. From that moment on, this Jewish feast of freedom took on new meaning in light of Jesus' death and resurrection. His paschal mystery ushered in a profound change in the beliefs and practices of the first Jewish Christians. Because of Jesus' paschal mystery, some rites of passage once associated with Judaism changed in Christianity. This was evident as the church no longer required circumcision for Gentile converts and allowed Christians to eat pork and other meat that Jews consider unclean.

Jesus' life reflected the fundamental attitudes of a faithful Jew who observed Jewish beliefs and practices. After his resurrection, early Christians rooted Jesus' teachings into the soil of Judaism and developed appropriate rites of passage consistent with his message.

Faith Formation

Developing fundamental attitudes consistent with faith happens in a cultural context. This begins at home and is affected by one's background and social context. The latter is especially significant in faith growth. Faith never develops in a vacuum but is influenced by family, friends, and social environment.

Generations ago, the church flourished in quasi-isolation from secular society. The latter's relativistic and individualistic norms were not as strong as today. Fewer things competed for people's time and talents. In this context, faith growth took a different focus than it does now. Today, for example, it's difficult to get the whole family together, not to mention gathering them to attend Mass as a family, as reflected in Rebecca's story.

> When Rebecca began parish ministry as a director of religious education almost forty years ago, many families attended Sunday Mass together. She remembers two families in particular. Both sat in the front pews. One had eight children, the other six. They were never late. How many families come together to Mass on Sundays today? Sunday morning work, soccer, baseball, and other pressures make this difficult. How can a family grow in faith and appreciate the value of faith traditions if it places little priority on Sunday Mass, other Catholic traditions, and prayer?

Fundamental attitudes and rituals influence faith. Regardless of our responsibilities, regular patterns of prayer and religious celebration are necessary for spiritual growth. Few religious rites of passage affect us outside of those we choose for ourselves. Hence, it falls on us to develop a prayer life that moves us closer to God.

THE MAIN POINTS IN THIS CHAPTER

Reflecting more deeply in light of the story of the old apple tree, we review now the chief elements that this chapter has considered. They can be summarized as follows:

- The story of the old apple tree is lived by every creature on this earth—plants, animals, and humans. All are engulfed by the cycle of birth and death, for everything is in transition; nothing stands still.
- All life serves as a meditation on our personal lives. The transitions occurring in nature remind us that we change at key life moments. As humans, we can know these changes, face them, and become better persons. Such transition times are opportunities for new awareness and growth.
- Each transition invites us to probe life's mysteries and see how God penetrates life's veil to disclose new insights into who we are and why we are here.
- Throughout history, civilizations have marked transitional times with rites of passage.
- Important life transitions, like birth, marriage, sickness, healing, death, burial, beginning an important journey, entering into war, and making peace are more than *mere events*. They must be *ritualized* or *celebrated* to recognize their full significance.
- Difference exists between the actual *transition time, happening, or event* (birth or death), and its *ritualization or celebration through a rite of passage* (baptism or a funeral rite).
- The wisdom gleaned from such ritualization tells us that celebrating events like birth, marriage, or other transition times through rites of passage completes them by taking

them beyond mere events and joining them to a deeper source of sacred power coming from God and mediated by a community.

- Ritual manifestations, like holding a sick person's hand or giving a hug to a hurting person, connect with the tensions experienced by sick or grieving parties.
- To walk in harmony with life, we move with the rhythms established by God for nature's good ordering.
- Outsiders do not always understand a culture's core message, because they do not understand the cultural values depicted or the rituals celebrated. When cultural beliefs shift, rites of passage also change.
- Jesus' life reflected the fundamental attitudes of a faithful Jew who observed Jewish beliefs and practices. After his death, early Christians rooted Jesus' teachings into the soil of Judaism and developed appropriate rites of passage consistent with his message.
- Developing fundamental attitudes consistent with faith happens in a cultural context. This begins at home and is affected by one's background and social context. The latter is especially significant in faith growth.

As a group, talk about this chapter, using these questions.

- What does the story of the tree and the dead branches tell us about transition times that we experience? What value is there in connecting such natural events with human experiences?
- To what degree do people today appreciate various transition times in their lives? How many people ritualize them through rites of passage and see them as opportunities for faith growth?

- Discuss the significance of ritual patterns. What do our ritual patterns tell us about life in general and faith in particular?
- Why is *story* valuable in probing into the ways that God deals with us? What do our stories tell us about ourselves?
- Cultures are delivery systems for the core truths that people believe and celebrate. Do you agree with this statement? Why or why not? Explain its significance.
- How do rites of passage connect with the Catholic faith? How do we liturgically celebrate various rites of passage?
- Pick out several transition times described in this chapter and consider developing parish and family rites of passage surrounding them. What would you include and why?

Chapter Two examines the impact of culture and community on transition times and rites of passage. It follows naturally from the considerations of this chapter.

CHAPTER TWO

Communal and Personal Perspectives

This chapter considers the impact of community and personal perspectives on transition times and rites of passage.

We begin taking a deeper look by

- → telling the story of the old toy case;
- → looking at life moments, the role of community, and earthly and personal connections;
- → considering Jesus as our model to imitate; and
- → seeing the community's role in faith formation.

Next, we examine main points in this chapter. Finally, we offer some discussion questions.

Take a Deeper Look

The *old toy case*, as the children called it, stood near the door of the small dry goods store. It was there when Joan started to work in the seventh grade and remained until the store was torn down. Generations of children looked yearningly into it and asked their parents for that special baseball glove, ball, whistle, or doll that occasionally appeared on the top of the other toys.

Children searched for new items in the case. Charles, the owner, closely monitored the number and kind of toys he bought, for his budget was limited and the money he spent had to produce a sale. Otherwise his take-home pay would be less for his family.

The front of the case was made of thick old glass, going back to the store's origins nearly sixty years before. Over time, it became dull. That did not stop the children from gazing into it while their parents shopped in the store.

As years passed, the glass wasn't the only thing that changed. The customer population shifted from middle class to poor. Even though the store survived the depression and the great 1937 flood, the challenges it faced became even greater. Many customers had little money, especially for things like toys. By the time Joan, Charles' daughter, began working there, the neighborhood was mostly African American. They were wonderful, hardworking folks, who trusted Charles and knew he treated them right.

In the store, customers were treated not like black or white people but good people who loved God and their families. They brought Charles chicken on busy days and asked for advice on business matters. He helped them, never taking a penny in return. The store was Joan's closest community, next to her family and church.

One fall day, a doll salesman came into the store. He represented a large firm in Chicago. Charles knew and trusted him. Since the store had a limited amount of space and a tight budget, the family needed to sell the dolls Charles bought at Christmas. Otherwise, they would just sit in the store and gather dust, making them more difficult to sell.

As Charles spoke to the salesman, he looked serious as he bought some dolls. When the salesman left, Joan asked what happened. He replied, "We talked about the kind of dolls I would buy this year. His company has a whole new line of them."

Charles said, "This is the first year they're selling African American dolls. He suggested that I buy some of them. I hesitated, because they are expensive and I wonder if our African American customers can afford them. Finally, I bought one black doll. I took a chance. Some of our white customers may resent the fact that I am selling black dolls. We may lose their business. But what is right is right and I'm going to try."

Joan admired her Dad's decision. She recalled an oft-repeated scenario, when she saw young African American girls looking into the toy case, gazing at only white dolls. They never said much, except "They don't look like us." In those years, if these girls were to have a doll to love, it had to be a white one.

In a few weeks the dolls arrived. There were five white dolls and one black doll. After Charles rearranged some merchandise in the toy case, he placed them there. Several weeks later, Sam, an elderly African American carpenter came into the store with his granddaughter. Sam was barely able to support his family with the money he earned. On this occasion, he asked Charles to show him work shirts.

While Charles waited on him, Bessie, his granddaughter, made her way over to the toy case. She saw the black doll and said, "Look, a black doll. It looks a little like me. I always liked the dolls in your store, but they were always white. This one is black. It's like me. I could really love it." The child kept staring admiringly at it.

When her grandfather finished and approached her, Bessie's countenance glistened as she said, "Look, Grandpa, a black doll. Isn't she beautiful? I never knew they sold store-made black dolls." Sam smiled.

The next day, Sam came into the store by himself and spoke to Charles. "All Bessie talks about is that black doll," he said. "It's as if seeing it unleashed something inside the child that freed her. I cannot afford to buy it at my salary. I wonder if you would give me a special price and allow me to give you fifty cents a week. It's early September, and I'll pay it off by Christmas." Charles smiled, and soon the deal was completed. By Christmas, Sam paid for the doll.

The week after Christmas, Sam came into the store with Bessie. She carried her doll. This gift from her grandfather went a long way to impress on this growing child that black girls, like white ones, can have nice dolls that look like them. Later, she learned that they can have whatever they work to achieve, just like white people. Not many years later, the civil rights movements of the sixties led to equal rights for Bessie and children like her.

> The experience deeply impressed Joan. She gave thanks for her father's courage that allowed him to buy this black doll. It made a big difference in the life of one black child. Although he made no profit on it, his real satisfaction was giving hope to this child and contributing to the real spirit of Christmas.

Bessie's freedom to have a black store-bought doll preceded the civil rights movement. What she experienced when companies began making black dolls symbolized a changing cultural context. Eventually this brought equal opportunities to all citizens, regardless of their color. The movement from pre- to post-civil rights days effected changes for African Americans. The doll story indicates that communities, as well as individuals, experience transition times.

Two factors influence the impact of transition times and rites of passage in any culture, namely, the community and persons within it. Throughout most of human history, the community took precedence over the individual. Community had a corporate identity that had to be maintained for the people's survival and growth. Individual rights, as we know them, emerged in the late Middle Ages. Both the community and individual play vital roles in transition times. When community identity is strong, people receive clear directions on how to fit in and contribute.

This also can be seen in comparing St. Mark and St. Alphonsus parishes. Both are about the same size and situated in the same middle class neighborhood that has seen the influx of many Hispanic and Asian peoples. The strong support of St. Alphonsus' members enabled it, under strong leadership, to reach out to the new members and bring them into the parish, when the style of the parish changed. This led to more vibrant liturgies, better catechesis, and a stronger focus on family ministry. This happened because the parish's previous commitment to social ministry enabled its leaders to apply to its own changing needs what it learned through a twinning project with a Central American parish. St. Alphonsus Parish remained a strong vibrant community that welcomed new members into it.

The opposite happened at St. Mark's. Weak leadership and bickering among parish leaders blocked any significant growth or admission of large numbers of ethnic minorities. The community suffered from a lack of vibrant ministries. As a result many parishioners left, often joining St. Alphonsus or other parishes. Some stopped attending church, and still others joined evangelical and other Protestant congregations. Energetic parishioners were blocked from accomplishing much in St. Mark Parish.

A community is affected by how open or closed it is to external influences. Before Vatican II, seminaries and convents were tightly controlled. Seminarians and sisters in training were not allowed to leave the grounds without permission. Frequently, access to television, radio, and newspapers was denied, and visitors were limited. After Vatican II, these restrictions were relaxed, and seminaries, and religious life began to be more open. Changing ritual patterns accompanied such changes.

This is evident in the way that prospective converts prepared to come into the church before and after Vatican II. Before the Council, the priest did most of the preparation, and the rite of passage that celebrated a convert's entrance into the church often happened in the church apart from the main Christian community. Today, the Rite of Christian Initiation prepares the catechumens and candidates, from the beginning of their initiation, in the midst of the community. This rite of passage culminates in a communal celebration at the Holy Saturday Easter Vigil Mass.

Every culture, parish, and family has a greater or lesser degree of openness. Before the 1950s, many aspects of United States culture were more closed than they are today. Families were more stable, civil law did not permit easy divorce and remarriage, and ethnic communities retained their separate identities. People usually worshipped at their own churches.

As United States society changed, secularism and materialism intensified, relativism and pragmatism grew, communities broke down, and individualism reigned. As this happened, the traditional Catholic lifestyle and ways of practicing the faith often diminished, lost their power, or were secularized.

Life Moments: Role of Community

God's call in the Old Testament is primarily to a community, not an individual. This began with God's call of Abram, "Go from your country and kindred and your father's house to the land I will show you" (Genesis 12:1). Abram's call was not to him alone, for God promised to make him the father of a great nation, God's chosen people. Abram obeyed and took Sarai, his wife, Lot, and others from Haran and proceeded toward the land of Canaan. From these origins, God formed the Jewish nation and made a covenant with them.

The covenant God made with the Jewish people reached its fulfillment in Jesus and the church that he founded.

Jesus brought salvation to the human race through his death and resurrection. This offer of freedom from sin and death is made to everyone, not a select few. To accomplish his mission, Jesus called apostles and disciples to share his good news with the world. He extended his first invitation to Simon and his brother Andrew, saying "Follow me and I will make you fish for people" (Mark 1:17). After Jesus fulfilled his mission through his death, resurrection, and ascension, he sent the Holy Spirit to his disciples on Pentecost. Through the power of God, this small band of Christians formed the church, a community of believers faithful to Jesus' mission.

This faithfulness is rooted in the community, under the direction of Peter, the apostles, and their successors. When speaking of those who heard Peter's message on Pentecost, Acts says, "So those who welcomed his message were baptized, and that day about three thousand people were added" (2:41).

Religious people throughout the world profess their beliefs and celebrate their faith in community. As St. Paul says in Corinthians, "Now you are the body of Christ and individually members of it" (1 Corinthians 12:27). We need community, for being human means needing others. We need one another for growth, survival, and to satisfy the deepest longings of the human heart. Without community it is difficult to celebrate in joyful times and to cope with sickness and death, as reflected in Sherry's story.

> Sherry stressed the significance of parish community to her adolescent son and daughter after they stopped going to church. She said, "Since I became Catholic, I continually receive strength from the parish community. Here, I attend Bible prayer sessions, study Scripture, and got much support at my father's death. Some of my best friends are parishioners now. I hope someday you will come to a similar appreciation of what the parish community can mean in your life." Sherry had an excellent relationship with her children, and they listened to her. Although they did not immediately return to active Mass attendance, they took her words to heart.

We develop rituals, including rites of passage, to help fulfill ourselves as humans. Rituals from various cultures illustrate this point. We see this in the vital role that celebrations play in native people's lives. Their rituals celebrate key life events and rites of passage. They celebrate coming to adulthood through adolescent initiation rites and marriage rituals. Their ritualistic celebrations often connect with the cycles of nature. These include rituals for planting and harvesting of crops and rites surrounding death. They also include celebrating with dancing, drumming, and chanting.

The meaning of rituals is connected with the history, beliefs, and fundamental attitudes of the communities that develop them. For example, the rituals celebrated by Jews and Christians have little meaning for those not professing these beliefs or those not knowing or accepting Jewish or Christian history and beliefs.

Rituals celebrating rites of passage also are affected by personal relationships. This became clear at an estate auction.

> The auction took place in a small town to settle an elderly woman's estate. The children in this family were estranged from each other. After the auction began, it became clear that intense jealousy existed among family members. Item after item sold for more than it was worth. Often a brother or sister paid two to three times its value to keep it from another sibling. The siblings bought many items this way.
>
> As the auction proceeded, many non-family members stopped bidding and left. Murmurs went through the crowd, reflected in words like, "Isn't it terrible what is happening. How can Elsie have such hostility toward her brother that she bids up the value of that lamp that he wants? She offered three times what it was worth until he stopped bidding," or "Why can't they let go of their anger for each other and mourn their mother's death? They just want to get even; they really don't want the stuff they buy."

An estate sale represents a significant life transition. While often difficult for family members, it puts closure on a loved one's death. Not in this family. Without knowing its history, it was impossible to know what really happened that day.

All communities experience transition times. For families, the death of a family member represents one such life transition. This happened when Olivia died. She was the heart and soul of her family. Healthy into her ninety-first year, she was the glue that kept them close. When she died, after the family celebrated at her funeral, it had to reorient itself to maintain their love in a new context. Eventually they developed new patterns to share their love, as they refocused family ritual patterns to keep connected.

Something similar happens in any community. When changes occur, it is imperative that the community involved develops new ritual patterns, as old ways die and new ones are born. With the closing of parishes and the formation of new federations from once independent communities of consecrated religious, the significance of rites of passage becomes more evident.

Earthly and Personal Connections: A Communal Context

Someone once said that to live is to be with. Relationships constitute the heart of being human. Without connections, we wither and die. The world of nature roots such human connections, which are filtered through the human community and reach their zenith in close interpersonal relationships. The interplay of earth, community, and individual came home in Isaac's time with native peoples. He recalled an experience with Harold, an elder of his tribe.

> As Harold and Isaac drove across the hot barren land near Harold's home somewhere in Wyoming, they discussed a problem that troubled Isaac. Coming upon a bluff overlooking a small stream, Harold looked up, pulled off the road, and stopped his truck. After a few moments of silence Harold pointed westward. In the distance a large bald eagle circled above the single tree

> that dotted the horizon of the rocky hills. He stared at the bird for about five minutes. His look indicated that he received the answer to his problem.
>
> Confident that Isaac did not understand, Harold explained that his ancestors, speaking through the eagle, answered the problem that he had with his son. Later, Isaac thought of how the solution linked his personal problem (his son), the broader community (his ancestor), and nature (the eagle).

As seen in the above story, three factors operate in any significant life change.

1. We are creatures of the earth. Life and death dynamics present in all nature pulsate through us. This helps us understand why some people return to creation to deal with personal life issues. This may take the form of admiring a newborn child or experiencing nature's beauty during a walk in the woods. Such earthly connections set the tone for other communications.
2. As members of the human race, we need community. It gives us the framework for healthy interactions. We develop friendships, marry, and work to accomplish our projects. At significant transition times we need one another.
3. We are naturally attracted to some community members more than others. The native man, Harold, discussed his concerns with Isaac as they drove over the Wyoming hills. Because of his trust, he shared his story with Isaac.

Community Connections: Mythical Perspectives and Rituals

For most Americans the land, earth, or environment that engulfs us is not grass or rocks, but computers, television sets, iPods, cell phones, Internet, and money. They are the backdrops for our initiation into life. Rooted in this technological soil, we grow and witness life's ups and downs. It's always been this way with humans. The culture where we are born and live sets the foundation for our attitudes and actions. The cultural context is associated with a people's mythos.

Just as the mythos of native peoples differs from that of average American city dwellers, so also the mythos of the following people differs:

- farmer and doctor
- teacher and student
- city dweller and rural citizen
- African and Australian
- Catholic and Jew

The mythical perspectives of various groups form the basis for their ritual celebrations. Thus, the ritual patterns of urban, white Americans differ from those of native peoples living on a reservation. The same applies to all groups and organizations, including families and parishes, illustrated in the following episode.

> When Rebecca became pastoral minister at St. Ann's Parish, she learned that the fundamental orientation of this parish was different from her previous one. One example was youth ministry. She was accustomed to a vibrant youth group, coming mainly from the large contingent of Hispanic youth who identified with the style of their parish youth minister. At St. Ann's parish, she was put in charge of youth ministry, which barely existed. Her previous parish supported this ministry. St. Ann's parish relied on the ministry at the local Catholic High School and didn't make it a parish priority.

A group's mythical patterns can be *functional* (business practices, accounting procedures, organizational skills) or *ultimate* (religious rituals, ways of expressing deep concern, funeral practices). Mythical patterns vary with different parishes, households and organizations. Thus, mythical patterns of one family differ from those of another. The same is true of parishes or business offices.

The mythos of a given group, people, or individual is the collective, fundamental orientation that sets the stage for the way that humans within that group respond to various life events.

Mythical patterns and their ritual expressions also differ. For instance, Catholics in Africa celebrate Mass differently from Hispanics in South America or Vietnamese in Asia. These differences carry over into United States parishes, as different ethnic groups enter the parish. Parish ministers have to reach out to encourage them to share their Catholic ethnic customs with the parish. Although their fundamental Catholic beliefs are the same, differences spring from their cultures.

Such mythical and ritualistic perspectives form the basis for how people celebrate transition times. For instance, Catholics believe in the afterlife and celebrate funeral services differently from persons who do not believe that life continues beyond the grave. Christians who believe that Jesus is true God and true man ritualize his role in the salvation of humankind differently from those who do not believe he is God. Something similar applies to belief in the Eucharist. Christian churches that believe Jesus is really present in the Eucharist celebrate differently from those who do not.

Individuals living in a particular family, parish, or region develop their attitudes and beliefs in line with the mythical and ritualistic patterns that they unconsciously accept. Their fundamental attitudes and beliefs influence how they respond to joys and tragedies. Today, functional or expedient answers to happy or sad events often replace ultimate ones. Rites of passage, if they exist at all, follow suit. This leaves those yearning for ultimate answers empty and unfulfilled.

> The fundamental values of a family or society impact their members, especially when they experience life transitions, like growing up or getting sick.

Mythical and ritualistic patterns never develop in isolation. They spring from the perspectives of people involved. This is evident when preparing for a special event, like a wedding or funeral. Engaged couples may have definite ideas on how they want to celebrate their wedding. Sometimes these differ from parental wishes or church policies. The issues concerned are real, for they flow from different mythical and ritualistic perspectives.

Community Connections: Personal Perspectives

Personal transitions always happen in a community context. When a child is baptized, family and friends celebrate. When a person dies, loved ones mourn. The church community needs to respond during such joyful and difficult times. How often do sick people or those who received a special honor get a card from the parish? The way parishes treat their members during transitions hints at their communal spirituality and effectiveness for ministry. When parishes reach out, they mirror Jesus' teaching that whenever they do anything for the least among them, they do it for God. The parish's support during good and difficult times helps greatly. This is reflected in the following episode.

> When a small boy died in a parish schoolyard, a large parish contingent immediately went to the boy's home, brought food, and provided needed consolation. At his funeral, the priest's homily and parish's outpouring of love blessed the family. Two weeks later, the boy's mother called the pastor and said, "If it weren't for the parish, I don't know where we would be today. Your love enabled our family to take our initial steps toward healing."

People who receive love from a parish during personal transitions see Jesus' love in flesh and blood. Nothing solidifies their commitment to the parish more than love received when they need it.

Jesus as Model

Jesus came among us as a Jew. He experienced transition times and rites of passage just as we do. We gain fresh insights into Jesus' redemptive activities by looking at them through the eyes of Mary, his mother. In so doing, we recognize God's fidelity as the backdrop for our salvation.

Jesus' family faithfully observed Jewish laws and rituals. His faithfulness to God remained steadfast through life. Mary anticipated his future challenges and knew the prophecies about the coming Messiah. Her faith consoled her and yet brought her much pain, for she knew her son had to suffer and die a cruel death.

When Jesus began his public life, opposition to his teaching arose immediately. Imagine Mary's consternation when Jewish synagogue leaders opposed his teaching. What was it like for her when such opposition began during his first preaching in the synagogue?

- Mary was a faithful Jew, and her son preached a different

message from many Jewish leaders. Was it not doubly difficult for her, as opposition to Jesus increased?

- Imagine her siding with her son against these religious leaders, as they called for his arrest.
- How did Mary feel during his scourging and crucifixion, as the support of religious and civic leaders and his followers vanished?
- Did Jesus' response to opposition from civic and religious leaders give Mary insight into God's workings?
- How could she understand why this was happening?

Nonetheless, Mary remained faithful. Perhaps Jesus' fidelity showed her that no matter what the circumstances, the only adequate response during traumatic life transitions is faithfulness to God. Jesus and Mary learned fidelity to God from Jewish history. Unlike some figures in Judaism, including King David, who were unfaithful, Jesus and his mother remained faithful during traumatic times. After the infidelity of Jesus' followers, his fidelity is an inspiring model for every Christian.

Since the risen Lord lives among us, Jesus' faithfulness and the church's compassion are bedrock for those who experience joy and sorrow. Christ is present in his body, the church. We are to follow him and remain faithful.

Faith Formation and Community

Faith formation never happens in a vacuum but in a given time, place, culture, and family. Its direction depends on the style of the group involved—whether it is open or closed. This is reflected in the changes that occurred in the Catholic Church during the last fifty years. These came about largely because of Vatican II reforms.

Prior to that time, the church was more closed to the secular culture and its ways of doing things. Catholics were citizens of this world, but many remained immune to its pressures. Powerful dynamics kept the Catholic conscience in tune with the church's beliefs and practices. The church taught love and the fear of God, but fear and guilt strongly influenced Catholic conduct. Fear of eternal punishment and guilt for straying from church teaching were powerful motivators to do right. The sacrament of Penance (Confession) was a strong incentive to stay on the right path.

> After Vatican II, it became important to consider how to minister at key life transitions, because the old ways no longer applied.

Such a spiritual worldview discouraged questioning. Catholics received answers to what was right and wrong from the church, usually from the priests and sisters. To deviate from church teaching in religious matters was considered sinful. To question implied doubt, which Catholics tried to avoid. There was little talk about ministering during key life moments. There were few sessions for young adults, separated and divorced Catholic groups, or bereavement committees. The Catholic community effectively initiated its members through its pre-Vatican II lifestyle.

With the changes at Vatican II, motivating forces of a relatively closed society disappeared. When the church encouraged Catholics to develop a mature faith, many Catholics began to question and doubt. In this context,

- Some Catholics no longer followed church teachings.
- The church no longer had the same authority over the Catholic conscience that she once possessed.
- The strong dynamics of the pre-Vatican II church disappeared.

As the church opened up, Catholics were encouraged to take their faith into the marketplace and act with charity and justice. As they did this, secular values often clashed with Catholic ways of acting. When this happened, a secular culture impacted the Catholic lifestyle and the secular culture often became the more powerful force in the lives of many Catholics.

Younger generations grew up learning the ways of the world. Even strong Catholic families have limited success in curbing this secularization of the Catholic mind, as secular priorities replace Catholic beliefs with many people. This often results in a loss of Catholic identity, as Catholics often become indistinguishable from their non-Catholic and non-believing friends. Many cease going to Sunday Mass and no longer follow the church's teachings on moral matters.

Previous rites of passage that once helped young people work through adolescence are now secularized.

The secularization of many Catholics seriously affects Catholic youth. With no adequate rituals or rites of passage to help them cope with the challenges of adolescence, some flounder, often experimenting with sex, drugs, and gangs. Adults often search in vain for ways to help them. Such help must be couched within a trusting climate, where young people feel free enough to be themselves and confident enough to trust adults who assist them. Similar dynamics prevail with Catholic adults. They need the church to provide a firm psychological and spiritual anchor to get them through difficult times. When adequate support is not there, many people leave the church.

In the open society where Catholics now live, community becomes increasingly significant. Searching, uncertain people need the support of a caring community. This starts with family and extends to friends and the parish. This means recognizing when people are going through transition times, as illustrated in the following story:

> The Jethro family suffered great trauma when Ellie, the mother, became seriously ill. She was not expected to live. Her sickness intensified the stress they were already feeling because the serious sickness of the eldest of their three young children. To cap things off, Ben, her husband, received a job promotion just before they moved into a new home.
>
> When their parish discovered their plight, families began bringing them food to see them through. The Jethro family appreciated this, especially since they knew few of those who daily delivered the food. This began while Ellie was in the hospital. Her recovery was slow, and parish members continued to bring food for two months.

The Jethro family will not forget such parish kindness. This story reminds us of the impact that a parish community has on the faith growth of parishioners. For this to happen, the church needs effective leaders to support its members in deeds, words, and sacraments. The church always raised up leaders as bishops, priests, and deacons. The sacrament of Holy Orders calls them to serve the community by providing leadership. Bishops, priests, and deacons proclaim Jesus' good news, lead the Catholic community, and preside at church sacraments.

- Their witness inspires parishioners to reach out to the needy and the world.
- They call the community to minister at key transition times through celebrating rites of passage.
- Their vocation completes the circle of responsibility first given to them at baptism.

Many challenges exist for the ordained clergy. When a man first expresses his interest in becoming a priest or deacon, the Catholic community needs to encourage and pray for him.

THE MAIN POINTS IN THIS CHAPTER

Reflecting more deeply in light of the story of the old toy case, let's review this chapter's chief elements.

- Parish communities, as well as individuals, experience transition times and changing rites of passage.
- Two factors influence the impact of rites of passage in a parish, namely, the community and persons within it.
- When family and parish community identity is strong, people receive clear directions on how to fit in and contribute; when community breaks down, rites of passage change focus and often lose their power.
- A parish community is influenced by how open or closed it is to external influences.
- As United States society changed, secularism and materialism intensified, relativism and pragmatism grew, communities broke down, and individualism reigned. Traditional rites of passage diminished, lost their power, or were secularized.
- From the beginning, God's call was primarily to a community, not to an individual. The covenant God made with the Jewish people reached its fulfillment in Jesus and the church he founded. Parish communities develop rituals, including rites of passage, to praise God, celebrate faith, and support one another.
- The meaning of rituals is connected with the history, be-

liefs, and fundamental attitudes of the communities that develop them. With change, it is imperative that communities develop new ritual patterns, as old ways of doing things die and new ones are born.

- The mythos of a given group, people, or individual is the collective, fundamental orientation that sets the stage for the way that humans within that group respond to various life events.
- Jesus came among us as a Jew and experienced transition times and rites of passage just as we do. We gain fresh insights into Jesus' redemptive activities by looking at them through the eyes of Mary, his mother.
- Since the risen Lord lives through the church, Jesus' faithfulness and the church's compassion are the bedrock for those who experience joy and sorrow.
- Faith formation happens in a given time, place, parish, culture, and family. After Vatican II, it became important to consider how to minister at key life transitions, because the old ways no longer applied.
- The impact of secular culture is the most powerful force in the lives of many Catholics and parishes today. Previous rites of passage that once helped young people work through adolescence are now secularized.
- The ordained are called in a special way to lead through service in the church.

As a group talk about this chapter, using these questions:

- Reflect upon several times that your family or parish community positively affected your life. Why were these significant times, and what lessons came from them? By whom did you feel supported?

- What does Jesus or Mary's response to Jewish law say to you? How do you see that their response to community norms can give consolation, hope, and strength to those who experience difficulties with church teaching?
- Discuss: "The response of a loving parish community or involvement in one can bring new direction to a person's life."
- How does human poverty symbolize the failure of Christians to recognize all people as brothers and sisters? Discuss ways that you have helped other members of Christ's body to deal with poverty.
- Why is compassion a necessary element of Christian community, especially in families?
- How do personal values and family influences affect a person's responses to transition times? Cite examples.
- Discuss the opportunities for Christian communities, especially parishes and families, to respond to joyful and tragic events. How do such opportunities offer occasions for faith formation?
- How do life experiences with nature help us appreciate some rites of passage?

This chapter has considered the role of the community and individuals in transition times and rites of passage. Chapter Three looks at the role of linear, cyclic, and liturgical time.

CHAPTER THREE

Time and Life's Transitions

This chapter considers time and its association with life transitions and rites of passage.

We begin taking a deeper look by looking at life moments or transitions in time:

- → addressing linear (historical), cyclic, and liturgical time by reflecting on the message of the wall clock;
- → considering time in light of Jesus as our model;
- → examining key aspects of what we have learned; and
- → seeing time in relation to faith formation.

Next, we examine main points in this chapter. Finally, we offer some discussion questions.

Take a Deeper Look

One afternoon in the fall, as I waited in line at our local post office, I glanced up and I saw a wall clock ticking down toward the New Year. This digital clock spelled out numerically the hours, minutes, and seconds before the new millennium would arrive.

As I watched the minutes decrease one second at a time, it hit me. Second by second we approach the new century, but we also come closer to our death. We count the seconds until the New Year, but the time of our death is unknown. Just as inevitably as the seconds on this clock count down to the New Year, they also indicate the limits of our earthly life. Every time I saw the clock in the post office, I witnessed the slow steady progress of my life and that of every creature on earth.

Life Moments: Transitions in Time

Linear, cyclic, and liturgical time offer different yet related perspectives. These ways of viewing time offer different windows to the world. We examine each one.

Linear Time

When I first saw the clock three months before the new year began moving toward a definite ending point, I thought of the steady march of time along a straight line to its end. *This straight-line time of our lives is called linear or historical time.* It moves forward second by second in a line that began when God created the universe. It continues until the universe ends. History relies on linear time. It is predictable, having a past, present, and future. We live, grow, celebrate, suffer, and eventually die in linear or historical time.

The religious significance of linear time took a new turn when God entered human history. God called Abram, telling him to leave his home and go to a land that God would give him and his descendents. In Genesis, we read,

> Now the Lord said to Abram, "Go from your country and your kindred and your father's house to the land that I will show you. I will make of you a great nation, and I will bless you, and make your name great." (12:1–2)

From that moment, human history changed forever. God's presence with Abraham and his descendents indicates the significance of linear time. Ever since this happened, God has been in communication with his people. God is not distant, but relates intimately to us. When Jesus came, he too entered our history.

Linear time is the way that Western civilization considers the endless movement of days and years.

To show the importance of God's dwelling among us in space and time, Jesus was born as a man. Speaking to Mary, the angel said,

> "And now, you will conceive in your womb and bear a son, and you will name him Jesus. He will be great and will be called the son of the Most High, and the Lord God will give him the throne of his ancestor David." (Luke 1:31–32)

Jesus lived among us and died to redeem us from Adam's sin. With his entry into history, salvation took a new turn.

The secularization of Western society sometimes makes God's presence difficult to appreciate. Take, for example, public education in the United States.

Over the years, Supreme Court decisions have separated religion and education in public schools. This follows from the interpretation of the separation of church and state that has been changing since our country's beginning. Some practices that were permitted for over a hundred years in public schools are no longer allowed. The education of many students often lacks roots that can only be found in values associated with religion.

What does this orientation offer to counter the problems around us, which include drugs, violence, and greed? Where are the rites of passage that help us during difficult times like sickness or death? Even in good times, this perspective inclines us to celebrate according to secular norms, focusing on worldly things.

Society's secular orientation carries over to everyday life. Take, for example, today's approach to marriages, even those celebrated in church. Many couples, while seeking a religious foundation for their marriage (or at least the desire to get married in church), are caught up in its secular aspects. They sometimes place high priority on such incidental details as finding a church with a long aisle. The secular approach to marriage points to a common attitude that fails to regard marriage as a holy covenant between God and the spouses.

Former rites of passage, based in religious values, helped young and old alike deal with life's transitions as they moved from one life stage to another. These rites have largely disappeared. Where they still exist, they have a secular tone. Without a spiritual base rooted in God, rites of passage have little value beyond celebrating secular moments or achievements.

In another vein, some people seek wedding partners through dating services, health spas, or country clubs. Others look for fulfillment in a comfortable life or status. At the end of life, every person has to answer the question, "What did you do with your life?" How many will say, "I made a lot of money, lived in a big suburban house, and had an important role in society"?

Ritualizing a superficial attitude helps explain why many Americans, rich by the standards of the world, are jittery and unfulfilled. Some live by the philosophy that "if my partner or job doesn't satisfy me, I'll get another one." When a secular orientation rules the day, unfulfilled people search for more. Often they do not know where to look.

Rites of passage need a spiritual base rooted in God.

A linear approach to time and history doesn't have to be superficial or functional. At his home in the Indiana woods, Bob watches the sun setting in the west and knows God is present in the movement of history.

> Sitting on the porch or walking in the fields, he hears the chattering of crickets and sees the penetrating lights of fireflies. Slowly, the sun's gold, purple, yellow, and red rainbow of colors disappears behind the hills as the light dims. The mystery of darkness gradually engulfs him. Within linear time, Bob experiences more than the secular. He finds a depth of beauty, meaning, and purpose that exists every second of the day. This hidden depth centers on the universe's spiritual nature, created by God, waiting patiently for us to find it. Here, we discover deep meaning, the foundation for religious rituals and actions that break secular bonds and touch life's core.

Past civilizations honored God's presence in the steady march of time. Some people get a glimpse of this inner world when they experience tragedies. The widespread trend toward fundamentalist thinking hints at people's desire to find basic answers in life. When mainline Catholic or mainline Protestant churches fail to meet members' needs, these members may turn to evangelical churches, as reflected in the following episode.

The answer to today's unhappiness can be found not by achieving more, but by going deeper into what we have.

An evangelical Christian church stands in a once-staunch Catholic area. This congregation did not exist fifteen years ago and recently completed a twenty-five-million-dollar addition. Many of its members are former Catholics, mostly under forty years of age.

They attend services there looking for a traditional message that links them with their Christian roots, especially Jesus. They desire a relaxed, welcoming community. They appreciate a worship space and rituals that help them connect the spiritual message that they hear each Sunday with the world where they live and work. They look for connections with like-minded Christians in multiple small groups that the church facilitates. Such evangelical megachurches satisfy some people, whose needs are not met in mainline Christian churches.

Life is more than a paycheck or affluent lifestyle. We look for ways to connect the everyday world with a more spiritual one, including God and like-minded Christians. In this search, some do not feel support from mainline churches, when they get little help in coping with materialism or dealing with personal, family, or work issues. If they are not fed spiritually in their churches, they may look elsewhere or drop out. Some Catholic parishes don't know how to address the exodus from their churches, especially among young adults. One wonders what is necessary to address the root causes for such defections from Catholic parishes. When

Pope John Paul II called for a new evangelization, he challenged Catholic pastoral leaders to consider the effectiveness of their ministry.

Cyclic Time

Linear time, with its focus on the continued progression of events through history, contrasts with *cyclic time. The latter refers to repeatable patterns of time involving events and persons that follow regular cycles of growth, decline, death, and renewal.* We see cyclic time manifested in creation stories.

> An Ojibway woman described her tribe's creation story of the origin of the great Turtle Island (America) and its inhabitants. She told of how the Sky Woman wanted to fashion the earth, but only water existed. She sent the three best animal swimmers to the bottom of the water to get mud. None succeeded. Finally, the lowly muskrat volunteered. Other fish and animals laughed at him, for muskrats were not considered to be really good swimmers. Eventually, Sky Woman allowed him to try. He swam and swam, losing breath at each stroke. Finally he reached the bottom and scooped up some mud.
>
> He had no more breath left. With great courage, he swam to the top. Reaching it, he died, while extending his paw to Sky Woman who received the mud. From it, Sky Woman fashioned Turtle Island, where all earth creatures now live. In getting the mud, muskrat gave up his life.

This creation story, like other native people's stories, tells of "beginning time," when God or God's agent created the earth and its inhabitants. Here, early cultures looked to find meaning. They returned to this beginning time each year and ritually celebrated the endless cycle of life and death. They believe that God gave their ancestors patterns to follow at this beginning time. God's directions continue through the stories passed down by the tribal elders in endless cycles of time. Their creation accounts contain key values disclosed by God in beginning time to be lived out in every tribe and by every person.

Beginning time was all-important for early people. They repeated the stories and rituals given originally to the ancestors. Knowing what happened in this beginning time was more significant than what happened at life's end. Linear or historical time made little sense to them, for

- they lived in cyclic time, reflected in the endless cycles of nature. It permeated all they did;
- they saw the sun come up and go down;
- they witnessed the moon beginning its sky journey with a silver streak in the heavens. Then, they saw it reach its zenith in the full moon, diminish, disappear, and rise again a few days later;
- they planted their crops by the seasons and watched them mature;
- they recognized life's cyclic nature in a woman's cycles. Their art describes a close relationship between creatures with cyclic lives. This is evident in a Polynesian painting that depicts the moon, a woman, snakes, bears, and other earth creatures that hibernate.

Their close identification with nature in an endless chain of repeatability led some to believe that God dwelled in sacred mountains that touch the earth and sky. Some associated these mountains with the largest tree in the vicinity, whose branches reached toward the heavens. This sacred tree was linked also with the totem pole in the center of their village around which they danced and prayed in circles and with the large tent post that held the hides that covered their dwelling places. Around this post they met as a family and prayed.

The cyclic view led some early communities to internalize their beliefs when they celebrated events like birth and coming to adulthood. When they did so, they professed the same basic beliefs and performed the same rituals. In so doing, participants learned about themselves and how they were to act. They repeated their rituals as they celebrated seasons and other events throughout the year. Such rituals left little room for superficiality.

The cyclic perspective was common in the cultures where Abram and Jesus lived. Gradually, historical perspectives entered, influenced by the Judeo-Christian belief in a God of history and a Savior who entered human history. A linear perspective grounded such beliefs, but the cyclic view often focused them through prayers and the liturgical calendar.

Early Christians incorporated both cyclic and linear elements into their belief and worship. This is exemplified in the way Jesus and his followers celebrated their feasts in ways consistent with cyclic time.

- Christians began the church year in late November, celebrated Christmas in December, and Epiphany in January.
- Lenten and Easter cycles followed a similar pattern. Priests and religious men and women prayed the Liturgy of the Hours in a cyclic framework.
- The hours of each day of the calendar year, from the first light of morning to the dark of night, set the tone for these prayers.

During the Middle Ages, the linear perspective gained predominance in the Western world. While maintaining the regular cycle of liturgical seasons, Christians moved into a historical mode of thinking and acting. This mode continues in our time.

Both linear and cyclic times are necessary for a healthy life. If a gap exists in present church attitudes and practice, it rests in the failure to incorporate the regularity of the cyclic into prayer and ministerial practice. Where this exists, pastoral ministers have an excellent opportunity to devise new ways to address the spiritual needs of parishioners.

Devotional prayers that encourage repeatable action, like morning and evening prayer, reflect a cyclic perspective. So do devotions like novenas and exposition of the Blessed Sacrament. Some of today's practices, reflecting the cyclic perspectives, are

- the daily and weekly celebration of the Eucharist;
- the Liturgy of the Hours; and
- rites of passage associated with baptism, marriage, anointing, and Christian burial.

Recognizing the value of cyclic time invites pastoral ministers to examine devotional prayer, as well as liturgical and ministerial practices. It also encourages them to incorporate cyclic dimensions into their lives. Concentrating on rites of passage affords a valuable perspective for doing this.

Parish pastoral ministers may be under the illusion that teenagers are not religious. In their busy lives, youth often put church attendance on the back burner. In the language used here, they live in linear time. What about cyclic time? In their own way, do they want to slow down? The following story addresses this question.

> Some parish youth group members expressed interest in having a prayer session, centering on Scripture. They asked to have it on the upcoming Sunday evening. The youth minister replied, "That's too soon. We need time to announce it, get it in our bulletin, and do the necessary advertising." The young people

> looked puzzled and said, "That won't be necessary. We'll get the word around to our friends." Reluctantly, the minister agreed. On Sunday evening over thirty teenagers showed up. Bewildered, the youth minister said, "I don't get it. We put up signs and spend weeks promoting a youth prayer night, and five youth show up. You pass the word around for three days, telling your friends there will be prayer with Scripture, and over thirty come."

What does this say to pastoral ministers? Perhaps, too much planning and organization may go contrary to the real needs and wants of many people, which are cyclic in nature.

Liturgical Time

The church celebrates the great feasts of Jesus' life in liturgical time. This consists of the weeks of the year, arranged around key moments in the history of salvation, like Jesus' birth, death, and resurrection. The liturgical year combines linear and cyclic time. From a linear perspective, it celebrates God's dealings with the chosen people throughout history, beginning with the call of Abram. God's fulfillment of his eternal plan in Jesus starts with the history of the Hebrew people. Here, God entered history and made a commitment to humankind, not as a distant God but as one intimately associated with us. The climax of this journey was Jesus' coming, his death and resurrection, and the birth of the church.

Each year, as Catholics remember God's plan of salvation, we consider our own salvation by recalling Jesus' dying and rising. His life challenges us to follow him, as liturgical time draws us more deeply into the mystery of God. In so doing, it balances the ongoing movement of historical time with the transcendent dimensions of cyclic time. What we call "ordinary time" thus takes on special significance.

Ordinary Time is the time between the major liturgical seasons of Advent/Christmas and Lent/Easter/Pentecost. While the name "ordinary" comes from the word ordinal, or *numbered* or *counted* time, the name in English reminds us that we work out our salvation in the ordinary events of life, as we work, eat, recreate, sleep, and care for our families. Sometimes, such events seem routine. Here, we mature, learn, and get old. As with the church's liturgical year, events interspersed in our ordinary time lead us to celebrate and mourn. These events may include birthdays, graduations, weddings, or funerals. Seen on a deep level, the church's liturgical year is a mirror image of our joys and sorrows. Jesus' paschal mystery, when he suffered, died, and was raised up, connects profoundly with the special transition times in our lives.

The above reflections focused on time. Regardless of whether we consider cyclic, linear, or liturgical time, transition times that Jesus experienced shed light on our own transition times. Hence, we look to Jesus as our model.

Jesus as Model

Jesus accepted his Jewish religion as a way of life. This included festivals, like Passover, and daily rituals involving dietary laws or prayers. Jesus never questioned whether he would obey such precepts. He observed the teachings and lived by the liturgical timeframe prescribed by the Law and Prophets. From childhood on, his parents and rabbis taught him about Abraham, David, and other great figures of his faith.

Surely, Jesus remembered the words of Ecclesiastes about there being a time for everything. He knew there was a time to be born and a time to die; a time to plant and a time to harvest; a time to love and be loved; a time to celebrate and a time to mourn, a time to speak and a time to be still (Ecclesiastes 3:1–8). Mary and Joseph first taught him such words of wisdom.

As Jesus grew, Mary observed how he integrated them into his life. She saw how the Law and Prophets became the norms by which he responded in good and difficult times. She recognized how he linked his mission with the role of the messiah and saw himself as the suffering servant of Isaiah (Isaiah 50:4–9).

Mary is also a model for us. Christian saints recognized her role in Jesus' life and invited her into theirs. As our mother, Mary is interested in how we fulfill the mission God gives us and is eager to help us.

Living amidst secular pressures that easily distract us from our true purpose, we need to appreciate how Jesus' fidelity to the liturgical norms of his Jewish faith gave him identity and purpose. They afforded him wisdom to recognize the implications of being God's Son. As a human like us, Jesus learned in the context of the times when he lived. We live in different times, but the responsibility to accept our calling is similar to that of Jesus. We are to be faithful to the vocation God gives us and to follow our faith, which gives us a sure norm.

Faith Formation and Transitions

To progress in faith personally, or help someone else do so, pastoral ministers need to consider the challenges and opportunities that our culture provides. To act as if we lived in Jesus' time does not work. It is no more successful than if Jesus acted as if he lived in Abraham's time. While faith's core beliefs remain unchanged, they need to be adapted to local times and circumstances. This is especially true in dealing with young people, not yet firmly grounded in faith. Pastoral ministers need to recognize that

- many youth have little understanding of what they profess as Catholics or why they celebrate as they do;
- they do not understand that baptism initiates them into a new way of life;

- they do not appreciate the Mass or Christ's real presence in the Eucharist;
- they associate the sacrament of Reconciliation with something they celebrated when they were seven years old and often do not understand its ongoing value, as they grow and face temptations.

Recognizing the significance of time in developing attitudes and beliefs helps us recognize that the time in which we live influences our spirituality.

Pastoral ministers do well to remember that growth in faith happens in linear and cyclic time. If cyclic time is brought into the equation, it can provide a needed spiritual focus. This cannot happen when time is reduced only to the linear or historical. Within history's ongoing journey, cyclic perspectives remind us that what happened two thousand years ago as Jesus walked among us still has significance.

Jesus' fidelity to Judaism's teachings and liturgical norms gave him an earthly identity. The same is true today when Catholics commit themselves to the teachings and mysteries celebrated in the liturgy. The parish community is encouraged to be involved in faith formation, for personal identity is found through a community. Without a communal connection, people move without a center. In Christianity, cyclic and linear time always have a center, who is Christ.

THE MAIN POINTS IN THIS CHAPTER

- The clock in the post office reflected the slow steady progress of the life of every creature on earth to a definite ending point. *This straight-line time of our lives is called linear or historical time.*
- Linear time moves forward second by second in a line that began when God created the universe. Linear time's religious significance took a new turn when God called Abram, telling him to leave his home and go to a land that God would give him and his descendants.
- The education of millions of students now lacks roots in deeper values associated with religion. Society's secular orientation often carries over into marriages, even those celebrated in church.
- We live, grow, celebrate, suffer, and eventually die in linear or historical time. Linear time, with its focus on the continued progression of events through history, contrasts with *cyclic time.*
- Cyclic time refers to repeatable patterns of time involving events and persons that follow regular cycles of growth, decline, death, and renewal. Early civilizations returned to this cyclic beginning time each year and celebrated ritually the endless cycle of life and death. Early Christians incorporated elements of the cyclic and linear into their belief and worship.
- Both linear and cyclic time are necessary for a healthy life. While the cyclic moves people into deeper patterns of thought and reflection, the linear can move to the superficial.
- Could it be that some young people need a more cyclic framework in their lives?

- The liturgical year combines linear and cyclic time. From a linear perspective, it celebrates God's dealings with the chosen people throughout history, beginning with the call of Abram and ending with Jesus' coming, his death and resurrection, and the birth of the church.
- Accompanying this progression forward to the end of the world and Jesus' Second Coming, we experience cyclic perspectives yearly as we remember God's plan of salvation.
- Ordinary Time reminds us that we work out our salvation in the ordinary events of life.
- Recognizing the significance of time in developing attitudes and beliefs helps us recognize that the time in which we live influences our spirituality.
- The larger community needs to be involved in faith formation, for personal identity is found through a community.

As a group talk about this chapter, reflecting on the following questions.

- Gather with a group of parishioners, friends, or family members and observe the movements of a clock from second to second, minute to minute. As you do, reflect on your life and how each minute offers an opportunity to thank God, glorify him, and serve our brothers and sisters. Use this as a basis for prayer and meditation, recalling episodes from your life and important aspects of your family. As you do this, connect your experiences with Jesus' life.
- Take time to read and reflect upon the call of Abram (Genesis 12:1–3), Samuel (1 Samuel 3:1–10), and the first apostles (Matthew 4:18–22). God calls you in a different time and place. How do these words apply to you, parish ministers, and parishioners? What do they imply? In reflecting on various *calls* in Scripture, remember that each one

involved joy and suffering. Apply these insights to your life and your parish.

- To better appreciate Jesus' presence among us, reflect on the following comment: "To underline the importance of God's dwelling among us, Jesus was born as a man, lived among us, and died to redeem us from our sins."
- Why do you agree or disagree with the following statement: "A linear approach to history does not have to be superficial."
- Comment on the following statement: "The answer to today's unhappiness rests not in achieving more, but in going deeper into what we have already."
- Discuss how the Catholic liturgy blends the cyclic and linear perspectives and the implications this blending has for parish liturgical life. How can a better appreciation of cyclic time help individuals and parishes probe more deeply into prayer and liturgical celebrations?

This chapter, centering on linear, cyclic, and liturgical time, sets the groundwork for a deeper consideration of faith, experience, and Jesus. Chapter Four looks to Jesus as our model. It reflects on significant transition times on his journey to free all people from sin and offer them eternal life with God.

CHAPTER FOUR

Experience, Faith, and Jesus

This chapter considers key issues in Jesus' life as seen through the eyes of his mother.

We begin taking a deeper look by

- → considering major events of Jesus' life by reflecting on the story of Lida and the picture of Mary holding her child Jesus. These events include: beginnings, changes, connections, joys/celebrations, loss, endings and new beginnings;
- → looking at Jesus as our model. We need God at every turn, miracles are possible, and no answer to life's mystery is worth considering without God.

Next, we examine main points in this chapter. Finally, we offer some discussion questions.

Take a Deeper Look

> Lida lived alone in the family home until her final sickness. Once, when a pastoral minister visited her, Lida told the minister that she was not afraid to die. Then, she looked down the hall leading to her bedroom at the picture of the Blessed Virgin and her child, Jesus, hanging on the wall. Lida had bought it years before at a parish sale. She said, "The other day, I saw an image of Jesus near the picture of Mary and her son."
>
> As Lida spoke about her eventual return to God, she assured the visitor that she was at peace. That afternoon, she impressed the pastoral visitor deeply with the power of her faith. After Lida died, her family knew that their mom died in union with Jesus. This filled them with hope.

We need to integrate faith beliefs with major life events, like adolescence, leaving home, and pastoral visits to elderly, sick, or dying people. Jesus experienced such events and gives us strength when we face life's transitions and minister to those who do. Mary had a powerful influence on Jesus' life. Her motherly love helped make him the man he was. It is fitting to begin our reflections on Jesus' life by looking at the events that shaped him through the eyes of his mother.

Imagine the depths of Mary's faith that enabled her to answer the angel at the Annunciation, "Here I am, the servant of the Lord; let it be with me according to your word" (Luke 1:38). The unique grace bestowed on her allowed Mary to respond in faith from the beginning to the end of her life. Consider this woman of faith, scarcely mentioned in the post-Resurrection accounts of the early Christian community, as a beacon of hope.

Her life inspired Peter, the holy women, and disciples to respond faithfully to Jesus' command to "make disciples of all na-

Mary was a strong faithful woman who walked through ambiguity and death with hope.

tions," even though this might mean their death (Matthew 28:19). Picture the scene when Mary was dying. View her with the beloved apostle and others in the Christian community. Imagine what Mary thought as she reflected on her son's life, joy, and sorrow and when she thought of the events in Jesus' life that brought salvation to the whole human race.

Life Moments: Major Events in Jesus' Life

In this section we examine Jesus' birth, adolescence, public life, last hours, suffering and death, resurrection, and the beginning of the church.

Beginning: Jesus' Annunciation, Birth, and Early Life

Any successful endeavor requires a good beginning. Beginnings promise new opportunities and root future success, reflected in the following story.

> The family of a child to be baptized sat in the front pew of church before Mass, with the small child in his mother's arms as the center of attention. His parents looked lovingly on him. So did the godparents, family, and anyone who walked past them. They sensed that something profound was happening. A built-in dynamism moved them to respond to his new life.

Like this child, the sprig of a new plant, the hatching of a sparrow, or the birth of a small calf invites those present to consider life in a new way. So does the bursting of a meadow into golden yellow, as the first waves of spring disclose anew the golden rods, whose seeds hibernated in the ground during the previous winter. The dynamics influencing the earth's response to new life are couched in the mystery of life itself.

Imagine Mary's reaction when the Angel Gabriel announced, "And now, you will conceive in your womb and bear a son, and you will name him Jesus. He will be great and will be called the Son of the Most High…" (Luke 1:32). Mary was the Mother of God. She was to give birth to a boy who was true God and true man.

As Mary lay breathing her last breath, reflect on what her memory of the angel's Annunciation might have been like. Jesus' birth was a pivotal transition time that the world had never known before and will never see again. Mary's *Fiat*, her "yes," made it possible.

What a powerful moment when God the Father sent his Son to humankind through the power of the Holy Spirit! Without Mary's consent, would the graces of redemption have flowed into the human condition? Would humankind have moved from the situation of sin, caused by Adam's fall, to the condition of salvation made possible by Jesus' redemption?

As Mary reflected on her life with Jesus, she must have centered on his birth. How proud, yet humble she must have been. She was God's faithful handmaid. Imagine, too, how as a mother she wanted the best for her child, but acknowledged that Jesus' life was not to be one of luxury. On the first cold nights after Jesus' birth, his warmth came from her with the help of castoff animal blankets. The beginning of Jesus' life reflected that of people on the run, rather than those living in affluence. As Luke says, Mary and Joseph "wrapped him in bands of cloth, and laid him in a manger, because there was no place for them in the inn" (2:7).

When Mary retraced her early years with Jesus, did she recall that the kingdom Jesus proclaimed had its earthly beginnings in her womb? In her last hours, did she feel intense joy knowing that she and Joseph carried out God's designs? No doubt, Mary realized that other beginnings in Jesus' life, especially his becoming a young man and starting his public life, were powerful transition times.

- How many times did Mary wonder why the twelve-year-old Jesus went off by himself in the Temple, thus worrying Joseph and her? She even asked him, "Child, why have you treated us like this?" (Luke 2:48).
- Did she reflect on what Jesus meant when he answered, "Did you not know that I must be in my Father's house?" (Luke 2:49).
- How often, too, did Mary ask herself why Jesus' words to her at the wedding feast of Cana seemed to have a sharp tone?
- Why did he say, "Woman, what concern is that to you and me?" (John 2:4). At the end of her life, Mary must have seen that every new beginning in Jesus' life was important.
- Then, imagine her joy as she remembered the hope she engendered in Jesus, the wisdom she shared with him, and the support she gave him during his life!

Jesus' life affords us a meditation on the importance of new beginnings and provides a model to imitate. His life reminds us to ask God for wisdom at life's turning points. Did not Mary often wonder "why" something was happening? From her, we learn to believe, even if we don't understand. As we turn to Jesus, we remember that just as Mary served him at every new beginning, she intercedes for us to God at similar times.

The above reflections invite all pastoral ministers to consider the opportunities for ministry at times like the birth or baptism of a baby, a marriage, or a graduation.

Changes: Jesus' Adolescence and Public Life

Jesus' coming to adulthood and beginning his public life were new starts for him. They brought significant changes and shifted his relationship with his parents and friends. Mary recognized this and adjusted accordingly. She prepared him well. Now it was his turn to fulfill his Father's will.

Jesus' home in Nazareth symbolized the poverty that was his life's fate.

At Jesus' baptism by John in the Jordan, his mother must have been close by. Did she recall Simeon's words that a sword would pierce her soul? When the crowds grumbled and sought to kill Jesus after he read the words from the scroll of Isaiah about the blind seeing, the deaf hearing, and the poor having the Gospel preached to them, what did Mary think? These words promised something new for humankind. Through them, Jesus set down norms for the salvation that he accomplished by his life and death. In Mary's heart, she already identified her son with the Suffering Servant foretold in the Old Testament. Sooner or later, it was inevitable that the full meaning of these words would crash down on her.

During Jesus' his public ministry, good and difficult days occurred. As his life changed, we hear little of Mary.

- Imagine how she stepped aside, but still supported him, and offered a mother's consolation.
- Imagine Mary's joy, when she saw huge throngs following him as he preached about God's love, repentance, and the need to love our neighbor.
- Imagine her joy when she heard Jesus say, "I am the bread of life....This is the bread that comes down from heaven, so that one may eat of it and not die" (John 6:48–49).

Mary witnessed firsthand the *something new* that Jesus' kingdom proclaimed. She found great consolation when he cured the blind man, raised Lazarus from the dead, and multiplied the loaves and fishes. How deep was the sorrow in her heart when many disciples walked away, refusing to believe Jesus' words about the bread of life (John 6:35)?

How did Mary feel as Jesus' time drew near and he journeyed to Jerusalem for the last time? At the Last Supper, Mary must have been there and recalled the meals she prepared for Jesus and her family when they had celebrated the Passover. Now, Jesus gives the world his body and blood as a permanent reminder of God's love.

Mark says,

> While they were eating, he took a loaf of bread, and after blessing it he broke it, gave it to them, and said, "Take, this is my body." Then he took a cup, and after giving thanks he said to them, "This is my blood of the covenant, which is poured out for many." (14:22–24)

Imagine what went through Mary's mind as Jesus spoke these words. During the next few days, she witnessed the accomplishment of God's eternal plan for the salvation of the human race. Reflecting on these experiences of Mary provides rich soil for pastoral ministers to apply the wisdom they contain to parish ministry.

As Jesus entered the Garden of Gethsemane, was not Mary close at hand? In the Garden, when Jesus reflected on his life and anticipated what was about to happen, he sweat blood. Did something similar happen to Mary? As Jesus asked his Father to take his cross from him, if it was God's will, what was she thinking? Did she hear him say, "Abba, Father, for you all things are possible; remove this cup from me; yet, not what I want, but what you want" (Mark 14:36)? We'll never know all the answers, but Mary surely recalled good and difficult times.

Loss: Jesus' Last Hours: Suffering and Death

Early church liturgies described Jesus' suffering and death as a *Felix culpa* or "happy fault." The *fault* refers to the horrible price Jesus paid for the sins of humankind. The *happy fault* refers to the reality that Jesus' suffering and death saved the human race from sin and reestablished it in God's friendship.

No liturgical expression can capture the feelings, thoughts, and actions that occurred during this important transition time in Jesus' life. Jesus' submission to his Father's will brought about a movement from sin to salvation. Mary experienced this stupendous event occurring in front of her eyes. She watched at a distance as Jesus was scourged and hung on a cross. Imagine how she felt when most of Jesus' followers, including Peter, fled! Imagine how Jesus felt! John says, "Standing by the cross of Jesus were his mother and his mother's sister Mary the wife of Clopas and Mary Magdalene" (19:25). A slightly different reading in Mark says, "There were also women looking on from a distance; among them were Mary Magdalene and Mary the mother of James the younger and of Joses, and Salome" (15:40).

Was the excruciating pain of the nails driven into Jesus' hands and feet any match for the pain that broke his heart in witnessing the defection of his followers? He preached to them for three years, yet they ran away in fear.

Picture the agony on Mary's face, when she heard Jesus cry out for a drink of water. Imagine the feelings that pulsed through her when Jesus forgave the good thief. Even in his moment of desperation, he reached out to the sinner. Imagine what she thought when Jesus asked his Father why he had forsaken him. The hours must have passed like eternities. Then, Jesus spoke to her and John. The Gospel of John says, "When Jesus saw his mother and the disciple whom he loved standing beside her, he said to his mother, 'Woman, here is your son.' Then he said to the disciple, 'Here is your mother'" (19:26–27).

When Jesus gave John to her and her to John as mother and son, Mary knew the end was near. As mid-afternoon arrived, Jesus' plaintive cry commended his spirit into God's hands. This marked the end of his earthly life and his return to the Father. His death effected a change in Mary's life and the life of every person. His paschal mystery is the gauge against which all human action is measured and the model beckoning every pastoral minister to *follow him*.

Just as Jesus' life changed as he grew, matured, and accepted his responsibilities to fulfill the Father's will, so every person changes.

At each life turn, Jesus needed the help of his Father, support of his mother and friends, and confidence that came because he knew he was doing God's will. So at each life turn, we need God's help and support from our brothers and sisters. Knowing this, pastoral ministers need a positive attitude, centered on hope and faith, which gives them confidence to bear whatever challenges they encounter.

Endings/New Beginnings: Jesus' Resurrection, the Birth of the Church

The death of my father and mother were the most devastating experiences of my life—even though I anticipated their deaths. When they died, I felt lost, alone, and empty. What my father told me several years before, when his health was good, was so true. He said,

> Many years ago, my father told me what I now tell you. "Stanley, some day I will die. No matter how hard you prepare for my death, you will not know what it's like until I die. Then, it'll strike you that you'll never see me again. For a while, you will wonder how you can carry on. It will be hard, but you will make it. This happens to everyone who really loves someone and experiences the person's death." After Dad and Mom died, I experienced the wisdom of his words. I also realized in a way that was new to me the importance of caring parish ministers who help a family deal with the sickness or death of a loved one.

My parents were elderly when they died. Imagine what it was like for Mary when Jesus died in the prime of his life, killed in such a horrible way. Her knowledge that he was God's Son made the pain more devastating. Mary's faith, hope, and trust allowed her to be the bulwark that the disciples needed to get through the horrible days following Jesus' death.

After Jesus' crucifixion his followers hid. They feared for their lives, wondering what would become of them. Did they ask whether the past few years spent with Jesus were worth it? They had given up everything to follow him. What did they get in return? Their dreams and aspirations shattered, they retreated in fear, as time passed slowly.

Imagine what it was like when Mary Magdalene went to the disciples' hiding place and announced that Jesus was not in the tomb. The spark of hope kindled slightly. Were the apostles afraid to think that Jesus had risen from the dead? They hesitated, for as Luke's account says, "But their story seemed to them an idle tale, and they did not believe them" (24:11). At that time, did Mary Magdalene or Mary, the Mother of Jesus, recall Jesus' words that he would rise on the third day?

Reflect on the joy of Jesus' mother when he appeared to the disciples after the resurrection. New hope entered the soul of Mary Magdalene at the tomb, the doubting Thomas, and the apostles on the road to Emmaus. After Jesus blessed and broke bread at the table with them, they said to each other, "Were not our hearts burning within us while he was talking to us on the road, while he was opening the Scriptures to us?" (Luke 24:32).

New Testament accounts of Jesus' resurrection testify that Jesus accomplished the greatest life transition in history. This was the Son of God's passing through death by rising again. All human actions are evaluated and judged in light of this passage. As our Christian faith says, "If we die with Christ, we shall also live with him."

Easter is the climax of Christian hope and the pledge of eternal life. From the beginning, the church has celebrated the Easter

We experience a difficult transition as we pass from this world to the next.

event as the center point of all liturgical rituals and personal spirituality. On this day, Jesus was raised up by the Father. In light of the resurrection, life on earth is only a way station on the road to eternity. Hence, when we make the most of our time on earth, every good deed we do here prepares us for a fuller life hereafter.

After Jesus' resurrection, he ascended into heaven. Luke says, "While he was blessing them, he withdrew from them and was carried up into heaven" (24:51).

- Jesus' work was complete. Now, his disciples were to carry on the work he began.
- His followers realized their responsibilities for the first time at Pentecost.
- When the Holy Spirit descended on them in tongues of fire, they changed and became strong, unafraid, and inflamed with the Holy Spirit. As the Acts of the Apostles says, "All of them were filled with the Holy Spirit and began to speak in other languages, as the Spirit gave them ability" (2:4).

On Pentecost, the disciples received insight and wisdom. They worked wonders that far exceeded what these simple followers of a man from Nazareth could do on their own without the power of God. They boldly proclaimed Jesus' message, converted sinners, and gave their lives in testimony for their faith. Imagine Mary's joy when she saw the fruits of Jesus' life and death! Is there reason to doubt that she was a central figure in the early church, bringing hope and consolation to Jesus' followers? After she completed her earthly life, Mary joined her son, as she was assumed body and soul into heaven.

Mary's Assumption reminds pastoral ministers that someday they too will enjoy eternal happiness with the Father, the Son, and the Holy Spirit. This is their ultimate life transition, as it was for Jesus and Mary. Eternity is the gauge helping them decide whether their present life path leads them toward or away from their final goal.

Jesus' resurrection and Mary's assumption remind pastoral ministers to assure grieving parties that deceased loved ones now enjoy eternal happiness with God. This gives consolation to living relatives and friends.

Jesus as Model

Major events in Jesus' life invite us to respond as he did during transition times. Like him, we need community comfort and support. His family served this role until he left home. Jesus' relationship with his mother was unique, and we can imagine their great love for one another.

> When tragedy strikes and little hope remains, the consolation of friends, family, and the parish are great gifts.

In difficult times, some friends remain steadfast in their love and others do not. When I was in an automobile accident and suffered a prolonged sickness, my parents, family, and some friends supported me. Other friends that I figured would be there for me, never came. I remembered this experience as I meditated on Jesus' last hours. As he hung on the cross, how did he feel when his disciples ran away? Could Mary understand why they were not there or was she too caught up in the drama to think such thoughts? Did she figure it out later? In my case, I eventually figured out that some people who stayed away were afraid or did not know how to act.

Was this true also of Jesus' disciples? Were they too weak or terrified? The sick person may be stronger internally than the healthy person who cannot witness the suffering of a loved one. From Jesus' last hours, we learn that nothing has to be done except to be present to a sick person. No other actions or gifts are necessary.

During transition times we need support from pastoral ministers. Following Mary's example, the effective minister does not lag behind, waiting for someone else to support the suffering person. They can show the way at various life transitions, like birth and death.

When Jesus was dying, his mother stood by his cross. So did John and Mary Magdalene. Religious art depicts them standing there. The flamboyant Peter and other disciples, who had not as yet internalized the meaning of Jesus' mission in humankind's salvation, ran away. Without this conviction, why should they remain to be crucified with him?

Mary Magdalene appreciated Jesus' role. Her conversion was profound, and her relationship with Jesus was holy. Besides believing Jesus was Lord, she cared for Jesus deeply and stood beside Jesus' mother at the foot of the cross. No one knew Jesus' role in the drama of redemption better than his mother, Mary. She must have realized the strong support that Mary Magdalene afforded Jesus. Imagine these two women as friends caring for Jesus deeply in different ways. The relationship between Jesus and Mary Magdalene is a paradigm of a healthy friendship between people, who know who they are, accept their roles, and commit themselves to serving God. Whatever one's state of life, healthy relationships are necessary. In times of need, they offer us a strong anchor.

In reflecting on Jesus' death it is clear that parish ministers cannot act like the disciples who run away. Rather, they are challenged to go out of their way to be present when family, friends, or anyone else needs them. Jesus taught us that the whole world is our sheepfold. When needed, our Christian vocation calls us to minister to the poor, sick, and needy and to develop an attitude that focuses on tragic situations.

Faith Formation

Pastoral ministers need a positive attitude to be effective. Without compassionate awareness and an eagerness to reach out to needy people, opportunities can be missed. Often, parish ministers miss them or make excuses, saying they have more important responsibilities. Such thoughts remind me of the time I anointed a dying man forty-six years ago.

> I sat in the driver's seat, ready to go to a city championship football game with friends on a Friday evening. The parish musician approached and told me that a woman needed to speak to me on the phone. I went inside and answered the phone.
>
> Maria, an elderly woman, was on the line. With halting words, she told me that Cletus, her husband, had just taken a turn for the worse. She said, "You'd better come right away and bring the oils to anoint him." I replied, "I plan to be there at 6:30 in the morning to bring him Communion." She said, "You'd better come right now." Everything human about me didn't want to go there that evening. I had anticipated going to the championship football game for weeks. I answered, "I'll come at 6:30 AM tomorrow. He'll be okay until then." She persisted in her humble way, "Father, I think you should come now!" Finally, I said okay. Disappointed, I returned to the car and asked another adult to drive to the football game. Then, I got the oils and went to Cletus and Maria's home.
>
> When I arrived, I was startled. Before that evening, Cletus had always sat in a wheel chair with a blanket over him. This night he was lying in bed, sweating profusely. He had no covers over him except a sheet. He was small and vulnerable.

> After a brief greeting, I began the anointing. As I anointed his head and proceeded to anoint his hands, death rattles came from his chest. I had never heard them before, and the gasping and gurgling are as clear today as they were then. As I finished the anointing, he stopped breathing and died.

I'll never forget that evening. Compared to it, the football game meant little. Thank God that I listened to Maria's entreaties to come and anoint him. I don't remember the teams that played football, but I recall Cletus and Maria and where they were in the room when God's special graces came upon us. That night changed me. It taught me to go out of my way to be present when people need help and to encourage other parish ministers to do the same. When I think of this episode, I understand why it was important that Mary, Mary Magdalene, John, and a few disciples were present during Jesus' last hours. I also see why Christians must be present when others need them.

THE MAIN POINTS IN THIS CHAPTER

- Joyful and difficult experiences solidify the need to integrate faith beliefs with major life events, like adolescence or leaving home, or pastoral visits to the elderly, sick, or dying.
- Mary was a strong, faithful woman who walked through ambiguity and death with hope.
- When tragedy strikes and little hope remains, the consolation of parishioners and friends are a great gift. During major life transitions it is critically important that we receive support from the parish.

- Most beginnings promise new opportunities and root future success.
- Pastoral ministers need a positive attitude, centered on hope and faith, which gives them the confidence to bear whatever challenges they encounter.
- Just as Jesus' life changed as he grew, matured, and accepted his responsibilities to fulfill the Father's will, so does every person change. Jesus' life reminds us to ask God for wisdom at life's turning points.
- No liturgical expression can capture the feelings, thoughts, and actions that occurred during important transition times in Jesus' life.
- The major events in Jesus' life invite us to respond as he did, when faced with our transition times.
- Jesus' Resurrection and Mary's Assumption remind pastoral ministers of the value of stressing the eternal happiness that a deceased loved one now enjoys with God. Easter is the climax of Christian hope and the pledge of eternal life.

As a group talk about this chapter, asking these questions:

- Reflect on times when community, including the parish community, positively and negatively affected your life or that of someone close to you. What resulted from these events? When did you get support from the Catholic community? What did you learn?
- Discuss: "The church as a community must be seen in light of Jesus' sacrificial death."
- Imagine what the Annunciation looked like through Mary's eyes. How did she feel? What implications did she see for her life and that of her son?

- Discuss Jesus' rejection by the Jewish officials and his followers as seen through the eyes of Mary, his mother.
- Imagine Mary's reaction when she held the dead body of her son. What does this say about Mary's love for Jesus' body, the church?
- Reflect on the hope that the paschal mystery of Jesus' death and resurrection, and the promise of new life, offer for those struggling with the loss of a loved one. Without belief in Jesus' resurrection and the promise of eternal life with God, what hope would there be for us?
- What lessons can we learn from the relationship of Jesus to Mary, his mother, Mary Magdalene, and John for our relationships? What do these relationships say about loyalty, friendship, and support?
- Discuss with a friend, group, or at a parish meeting the statement: "A positive pastoral attitude is necessary for a solid ministerial response."

This chapter suggested key transitions in Jesus' life as models to imitate during transition times. It completes Part One and sets the stage for consideration of specific life transitions, treated in Part Two.

PART TWO

Rites of Passage: Opportunities for Faith Formation

On a cool November day, Fr. Jim arrived at the hotel next to the airport after a diocesan conference for Catholic leaders. As he looked toward the airport, he saw thirty or so military men and women in fatigues standing outside the lobby. Sensing they were going overseas, he went outside to thank them. Because he was wearing his black suit from the conference, they recognized him as a priest. He introduced himself, asked their names, and thanked them for their service to their country.

Upon hearing that Fr. Jim was from Toledo, they said one of their company was from that city, too. The man, Jason, was not outside, and several soldiers went to find him. Jason then introduced himself. Eager to touch base with someone from home, Jason indicated where he lived. Fr. Jim knew his grandmother and assured him that he would pray for him.

The next day, when Fr. Jim flew out of this small airport, he witnessed a beautiful ritual created by local townspeople. Since the airport was a main staging area for troops going to and returning from overseas, local people committed themselves from the beginning of the Middle East war to be there every time a plane returned or left for military duty. Ten to thirty

> townspeople, standing on both sides of the ramp to the plane, formed a human tunnel, as the troops arrived and left on each flight. They shook the hands of each military man and woman, expressing God's blessings and their thanks. They also stocked an airport store with food, snacks, and various sundries for them to take on their travels or use while at the airport. After returning home, Fr. Jim contacted Jason's father, who was very grateful.
>
> Standing in the airport that day, Fr. Jim saw what a traumatic life transition it was for men and women, like Jason, who leave for an uncertain location. Often, it's the first time they've been out of the country. This means leaving a spouse, children, and other loved ones. It involves stepping into the unknown, wondering if they will return.

Many of the townspeople in the above story were Christians. This ecumenical group banded together to reflect the heart of Jesus' message of love, support, and compassion. The motivating force of such Christian efforts centers on sharing Jesus' good news in words and deeds. This is important during transition times, when caring community impacts positively on people's lives.

When a parish, family, or Catholic organization supports us, we witness God's love in action. This happened after a tornado in the Cincinnati area. After it devastated a western section of the city, Catholic high school students, wearing their school sweatshirts, assisted throughout the area. They volunteered to fix fences, assist the elderly, pick up debris, repair doors and windows, and bring food and water to the needy.

It's been years since this happened, but area residents still talk about the Catholic students who made a difference. During this difficult time, as citizens began to rebuild their lives, these young

Catholic men and women provided living examples of faith. They influenced the physical and spiritual life of those they helped and provided a solid testimony of love.

> The Christian community can serve as a powerful witness of Jesus' good news.

These two episodes introduce the life-changing transition times that we explore in Part Two. During Jesus' final hours on earth, imagine how he felt when most of his disciples abandoned him. This abandonment challenges us not to be like them when people are in need. Rather, we are to walk in the footsteps of Mary, John, and Mary Magdalene and support others who stand in the shadow of Christ's cross, regardless of what it entails. In such times, people need us to sustain them.

Response to any significant life transition involves three factors, namely: the *beliefs or faith* of those involved, *ritual* response, and *action* concurrent with and following the life event. Our *beliefs* affect how we respond during life's changes, which are ritualized differently from person to person. The death of a parent of a believing family evokes the hope of eternal life for the deceased loved one. Non-believers will not have the same response. A believer *ritualizes* death with communal and individual support and prayers. Changing *action* patterns accompany transition times. After the death of a parent, families often change their lifestyles. Something similar happens to others during transition times. The three factors of belief, ritual, and action are present in every major rite of passage.

Belief

The significance of *communal or personal belief* is illustrated in the following story.

Gertrude's death happened peacefully and without fanfare. Her husband had died years before. Her only son, Mike, expected it. Nonetheless, he grieved terribly. During the wake, he kept saying, "Mom's gone forever. I'll never see her again. Where is she?" After hearing these words, the parish bereavement minister asked Deacon Ed to speak to him.

Mike was uneasy when the deacon approached, for he was not a practicing Catholic. He claimed no church allegiance and sometimes questioned God's existence. After they spoke for some time, Deacon Ed said, "Mike, be at peace. Your mom's suffering is over. It's hard, for you loved her very much and took good care of her."

Mike replied, "That's fine, Deacon Ed, but she's gone forever. She is no more, is she? If so, where is Mom?"

The deacon answered, "Our Christian faith tells us that your mother now enjoys eternal happiness with God. Have faith in Jesus. He will raise up your mom after death to live forever with him in heaven. Your mom believed and died with Christ. She is now with him in heaven. You are the one that suffers, not her."

When Mike heard Deacon Ed's words, it seemed as if he heard about eternal life for the first time. Even though he learned about it growing up, it never sank in until after his mom died. He said to Deacon Ed, "Do you really believe she is happy? If so, I can be at peace." As Mike said this, his eyes filled with tears. God gave him the grace to believe again, brought about by his mom's death and the words of Deacon Ed.

In joyful times we have recourse to faith to show our thanks. Just as Thanksgiving is a national holiday in the United States, so the virtue of thanksgiving is integral to Catholic belief and practice. We are reminded of this every Sunday, as we gather for the Eucharist. Joyful times remind us that all we have and are comes from God. With God's grace, our parents birthed, sustained, and supported us. We too must do the same for others, as we give thanks.

During transition times, belief is an anchor to sustain us. Believing in other humans comforts us and believing in God gives us purpose. Belief makes a difference when faced with ultimate aspects of life, like birth and death. The believer's faith enables one to transcend this present life and look forward to a life to come. A person with no belief in the afterlife must make sense out of this present life and of our ultimate destiny in some other way. This is hard to do, amidst the pain and injustice we endure.

Catholics believe in the Trinity, Jesus, church, Scripture, moral law, and the sacraments. Christians rejoice and suffer with Christ during life's transitions. We join our faith with others to appreciate life's purpose in light of our beliefs. Faith is our lighthouse on our journey to eternity. Recognizing the importance of belief during life's transitions underlines the importance of sharing these beliefs. In so doing, faith becomes a central focus when dealing with people who are experiencing joys and sorrows.

Ritual and Prayer Response

We celebrate joyous times, like baptism and marriage, and we support each other in difficulties by attending wakes and funerals, bringing food to grieving people, and giving them time to mourn. We mark transition times with rituals. We celebrate the transition times associated with our faith in the same way. We ritualize the birth of Christ with prayers, Christmas cribs, and liturgical celebrations. We remember Jesus' saving actions during Lent, Holy Week, and Easter. Such celebrations indicate the significance of communal rites of passage.

Ritual and prayer response is a normal activity of believers.

Pastoral ministers must be sensitive to transition times and the community needs to respond with faith and rituals, as reflected in the following episode.

> When I arrived to say the prayers at Matilda's wake right before the viewing ended, the undertaker said, "Father, I am glad you came." I was alone with him in the room. When I asked who paid their last respects, he said, "Look at the visitor's book." As I did so and signed the page, my name was the only one there.
>
> The next morning, when I celebrated Matilda's Christian Mass of Resurrection, I was the only one in church besides the undertaker. Even the servers forgot to come. This memory remains permanently etched in my mind as a sad example not to be repeated. Transition times must be ritualized. This is the human and Christian thing to do.

Christians ritualize life transitions with prayers, which ask God to give people courage and hope. All transition times look to the future, which we sometimes face with trepidation. When returning home from military service, assuming a new leadership role, getting a divorce, or having a miscarriage, people need to be encouraged to go forward with hope. In such circumstances, we need prayer support. Above all we need God's assistance. Often, such prayers ask for God's help, as we invoke God's protection for loved ones who leave for college or ask God's help for a sick child.

Of course, we don't just ask God for things. We praise, honor, thank, and worship God for what we received. In such joyous transition times, we give thanks. While admitting our unworthiness, we better appreciate the blessings we received.

Concurrent and Subsequent Action

Transition times require *concurrent and subsequent action.* When we choose a new life state, like marriage, we assume responsibilities flowing from our choice. Marriage and parenthood bring a shift in attitudes and patterns of living. The same applies to choosing to go to college instead of getting a job. Each new life change requires new action patterns.

Remembering the importance of belief, ritual, and action during transition times helps us respond in loving ways.

Transition times over which we have little control also require a change of action. When soldiers are seriously wounded in war and never walk again, their emotional scars may be as difficult to bear as their physical ones. The same is true of any sickness that radically changes our life.

Part Two is divided into five chapters. Each treats a key life transition, like beginnings, changes, joys/celebrations, tragedies, and endings/new beginnings. The chapters

- start with a life experience, like birth;
- analyze the experience in light of faith, indicating how Jesus' life offers a model to imitate;
- consider the life experience as an opportunity for faith formation;
- summarize main points treated in the chapter; and
- offer questions and suggestions to talk about the contents of the chapter.

CHAPTER FIVE

Beginnings

This chapter considers beginnings and discusses significant rites of passage that provide opportunities to share Jesus' love.

We begin taking a deeper look by

- → telling the story of spring in the country;
- → looking at beginnings;
- → considering Jesus as our model to imitate; and
- → recognizing beginnings as opportunities for faith formation.

Next, we examine main points in this chapter and then offer some discussion questions.

Take a Deeper Look

> Spring is a wonderful time in the country. Each year, the red bud trees invite us to experience new beginnings. When Sherry sees them in full flower, she knows that soon the grass will need cutting. Before long, new green shoots jump from the earth as the honeysuckle vines protrude onto the road across the dam of the lake. Snakes appear around the water and newly born deer cuddle in beds of tender fresh grass. From these small beginnings, the earth rapidly blankets itself with new plant and animal life. The endless cycle of birth, growth, and maturity continues anew.
>
> This panorama unfolds as Sherry watches it from her front porch or through the picture window facing the woods. When she walks the trails in the back woods, a symphony of new life bursts forth everywhere. Wildflowers vie with weeds to cover empty spaces on the earth's floor, and baby birds, rabbits, squirrels, coyotes, and bugs show themselves along the land's crust.
>
> As Sherry walks, she asks herself, "How is this new life different from the life that comes with a baby's birth or an adult's new beginnings, as they move locations, get sick, recuperate, find new friends, and marry? What difference is there between nature's cycle of birth and death and that which occurs in humans?"

Tropism and instinctual behavior regulate nature's cycles. Birth and death are natural to this process, and although humans experience them, we differ from the rest of earthly life. Our ability to form concepts, to reason, and to act freely makes us unique and reflects our spiritual nature. Reason enables us to replay past experiences, weigh their pros and cons, and learn from them. It allows us to develop science and technology, which are not possible for other earthly creatures.

> Without the orderly patterns that nature provides, the earth would fall into chaos.

Our rationality helps us see future implications of our actions at key life moments. This happened when Fr. Jim talked to the service men and women awaiting their departure for military service. While indicating their apprehension in leaving their loved ones, they also manifested pride and enthusiasm, for they embarked on a mission to help our country and liberate oppressed people. Because people can see the implications of their actions, they need love, encouragement, and support during transition times, like birth, leaving for military service, college, sickness, and death.

Life Moments: Beginnings

> The year before my mother died, she asked me to go through her hope chest with her. As we took out item after item, she told me each one's history. When we got to the bottom, we found a pack of old cards, neatly arranged with a string holding them in place. I slipped out one card. The two-cent first-class stamp indicated its age. Noticing the date of February 8, 1934, I perked up. I was born on February 2, 1934. The card to my mother at Good Samaritan Hospital, Cincinnati, Ohio, was from my Dad.
>
> The card had a picture of a puppy on the front. Inside were the handwritten words, "Doggone it, hurry up and get well, so that I can take you home."

> It also contained a safety pin attached to a piece of white cardboard with the words, "Something useful with which to pin baby diapers on. If the pin doesn't work, try this chewing gum!" An old stick of Wrigley Brothers chewing gum was still inside the card.

Birth, a fundamental human experience, has always been surrounded by rituals, mostly of a religious nature.

Finding this card connected me to my roots. After reading it, I recalled a photo taken during my parent's visit to my uncle Louis, a seminarian studying to be a Maryknoll priest. The picture showed Dad and Mom sitting on the ledge of a large fish pond. Mom was pregnant. It struck me that I was in her womb. This picture touched a deep core inside me, for it reflected an early stage of my life. Such memories move us to consider life's origins. In our antiseptic world we many never reflect deeply enough on the mystery of birth. Failing to appreciate our core experiences makes it more difficult to appreciate life itself. The fact that many birthing mothers spend less time in the hospital, use modern conveniences, and return to their secular jobs soon after giving birth doesn't minimize the power of this birthing event.

When seeing a newborn child, how can we doubt that God is the ultimate source of life? Instinctively, parents know their child's birth is special, but still need help to sift out the event's spiritual implications involved in their responsibilities of helping their child grow in love of God and neighbor. Parishes can help parishioners appreciate the spiritual implications of birth. They can take their lead from secular advertisers, who make the most of birth for monetary gain. The product division of a major company considers a child's birth as a major *entry point* for their products. After a woman gives birth, parents receive free baby samples and other materials describing the "latest products that bring children health and happiness." These often take the form of powders, shampoos, clothes, and health items. Before leaving the hospital, women receive complimentary literature, describing the latest in baby cleanliness and health.

Pastoral ministers can learn from this business approach by acknowledging a child's birth as a special time to grow in faith. In so doing, they recognize a child's birth as a *spiritual entry point* that parents and children share with the Christian community.

Each new beginning, like marriage or a new job, can invite us to grow in faith.

Since the built-in mechanism to move forward is sometimes daunting, we sometimes recoil from new challenges. New beginnings involve letting go of the old and starting anew. *Such challenging times include a degree of vulnerability as we walk into the unknown.* They are times of growth, and if we do not grow, our lives wither and die. In this regard, a newly married couple, unwilling to refocus their individual lifestyles, has little chance for a happy future. A business owner, unwilling to use the opportunities made possible through mechanization, computer technology, or robots, runs the risk of failure.

In contrast, parish leaders can take leadership in connecting core religious truths with changing circumstances. If they do not, some parishioners will seek spiritual nourishment elsewhere. Embracing new options means meeting new people. As this happens, when we face new challenges, the values learned in childhood strengthen us. The following episode makes this point.

> Mark attended a summer conference for high school honor students several hundred miles from his home. This was the first time he was away from home overnight. The two-week program took place

> in a military-style facility with five students staying in each cabin. The sessions were highly competitive and stressful. Mark's chief stress came from other students in his cabin. They had different values from his. They cursed and used crude language.
>
> One was the ringleader, and the others went along, afraid to challenge him. They soon realized that Mark did not mimic their crude language and obscene jokes. In the cabin, he mostly stayed to himself. Sensing this, the ringleader made fun of him, and the others went along. It was an uncomfortable experience.
>
> Mark looked forward to the last day of the conference. When it came, he hurriedly packed his belongings. As he did so, the ringleader walked into the cabin. Mark said "Hello," as he had each time that he saw him. The other youth stopped and said, "I've got something to tell you. I apologize for the way I treated you. You might think that I respect the other guys who went along with my crude language. If you think this, you're wrong. I have little regard for them. The only person that I respect is you. You were true to your values. All week, I wondered what makes you tick. I tried to change you, but I really wanted you to stay firm in your positive ways. You did."
>
> "When I leave here today and begin my last year in high school, I plan to reexamine my values. Your actions challenge me to grow up. Thanks for being true to yourself."

Mark never realized until then what a positive influence he had on this young man. Reflecting on this story can help pastoral ministers recall how challenges always exist with new beginnings, especially if they involve separation from family and friends. The episode also illustrates the importance of advising young people, when they go away from home, that they may be challenged, morally and in other ways.

Jesus as Model

Imagine what Jesus' birth meant from Mary's perspective. The angel's first announcement of Jesus being the "Son of the Most High" must have kept ringing in her ears during the nine months that followed (Luke 1:32). Imagine how this affected a girl who was only in her early teens. Like any mother, she wanted the best for her son. How many times did she recall the ancient prophecies foretelling his birth and death? What did they tell her in anticipation of his arrival?

- Picture Mary's disappointment in learning that she, Joseph, and Jesus had to make the arduous trip to Bethlehem.
- Consider her feelings when learning there was no room at the inn and her concern when she and Joseph moved to a stable.
- Did not her anxiety turn into joy when Jesus was born and she held him in swaddling clothes? At that moment, where he was born took a back seat to holding the Son of God safely in her arms.

Mary gave the world the gift of incarnate love. The overwhelming mystery of God-with-her strengthened Mary to face possible capture by Herod, and the Holy Family's flight into Egypt. Jesus' birth into the world places every child's birth in a new light. His birth glorified the miracle of birth and invites parents to see their child's birth as an unmatched spiritual event. Nowhere else do the divine and human touch any more powerfully than they do at this time. Jesus' birth is called *the Incarnation*. In a sense, every child's birth is an incarnation—an enfleshing of God's love in a newborn child resting in a mother or father's arms.

Just as the angels, shepherds, and Magi celebrated Jesus' birth (Matthew 2:1–12), so do parents celebrate their child's birth. Every newborn child deserves reverence as an incarnation of God's love. Seen in this light, the best gifts parents give their children are spiritual ones, like love, devotion, and prayer. What is better, a Mass offered for a child's health or some designer underwear? What is better, a spiritual symbol, like a crucifix or a plaque for the baby's room, or a toy? Jesus received gifts of gold, frankincense, and myrrh, but the best gifts he received were spiritual ones.

Was there ever a more powerful expression of love between Mary and Jesus than the moment when she looked at him immediately after his birth?

Many new beginnings occurred in Jesus' life. Imagine how these looked from Mary's vantage point. After Jesus' birth, the Holy Family went to Egypt, then to Nazareth. When Jesus was twelve, they journeyed to Jerusalem to celebrate the Passover. At that time, how did Mary feel when Jesus said that he had to be about his Father's business? Did his words remind her that in a few years he would leave home to begin his life's task? Consider how Mary's feelings intensified when Jesus was baptized by John in the Jordan. What did she think if she was there and heard the voice from heaven saying, "You are my Son, the Beloved; with you I am well pleased" (Luke 3:22).

At the beginning of Jesus' public life, he gathered a community of disciples who constituted the foundation of his future church. These early leaders followed him until the end, when most of them abandoned him. This reminds modern disciples to support those in need especially during tough times. To address new beginnings we look at two virtues in Jesus' life, trust and humility, as seen through Mary's eyes.

Trust

As Jesus began his public life and gathered his disciples his trust in God never wavered. His life reflects the words of Psalm 119, "Let your steadfast love come to me, O Lord....Then I shall have an answer for those who taunt me, for I trust in your word" (verses 41–42).

- Jesus showed great trust in his Father when he forgave the paralytic man's sins and raised him from his stretcher (Matthew 9:2–8).
- He manifested a similar trust during the multiplication of the loaves and fishes and while curing the Samaritan's daughter (John 6:1–9). Never did he doubt that God was with him, even when his disciples walked away, after he promised to give them his flesh and blood to eat and drink (John 6:66).
- During his darkest hours, as he sweat blood in the Garden of Gethsemane, doubts entered his mind, but his trust never wavered. He said, "My Father, if it is possible, let this cup pass from me; yet not what I want but what you want" (Matthew 26:39).

At every beginning in Jesus' life, Mary's amazement must have grown as she witnessed Jesus' trust, when he taught, cured, and ultimately gave his life on the cross. Did not his example buoy her up and reinvigorate her confidence, especially during the darkest hours of his agony and death? What was it like for the mother of God's Son to stand by helplessly as Jesus was brutally executed? Imagine what it took for her to maintain trust in God during this ordeal!

As we ponder Jesus and Mary's trust, we come to see the importance of trust in God during life's beginnings, even when these bring suffering and disappointment. Every person needs trust when a loved one dies. Imagine also the trust required of a young couple who gives birth to a deformed child and take him home to begin a radically different life from what they knew before. Without trust in God what is left to hope for at such times?

We need to trust during beginnings, like winning a college scholarship or suffering a tragedy. Jesus is our model. If we join our beginnings with his, we become confident of ultimate victory. This was Jesus' way, and we are invited to follow him.

Humility

Humility enables us to know who we are and respond accordingly. It acknowledges our humanity and our personal gifts. Mary realized her blessings as the Mother of God and did not brag about her upcoming motherhood. Jesus lived a humble life as a child in the small village of Nazareth. He could have come as a king, ruler, or military commander, but chose none of these. Instead he remained unnoticed by the outside world as he grew into manhood. His humility is evident as he goes through the countryside and proclaims the kingdom of God, heals the sick, raises the dead to life, and teaches a message of justice, love, and forgiveness. Mark says,

> When they had crossed over they came to land at Gennesaret and moored the boat.... And wherever he went, into villages or cities or farms, they laid the sick in marketplaces, and begged him that they might touch even the fringe of his cloak; and all who touched it were healed. (6:53–56)

Jesus roots humility in trusting God. The New Testament reveals Jesus' humility and tells us that the divine creator of all things loved us so much that he gave his only Son to save us. As Paul says, "But God proves his love for us in that while we still were sinners Christ died for us" (Romans 5:8). The mystery of our

> The deepest fruits of humility spring from faithfulness to God, not from us.

salvation rests in Jesus' humility. He fulfilled God's plan without fanfare or asking anything in return but love. Would we have imagined that the people he came to redeem, including you and me, would turn on him through sin? We could not figure out alone that in spite of our unfaithfulness, God forgives us again and again, if we are sorry.

Jesus is the model of humility for all. He says,

> Take my yoke upon you, and learn from me; for I am gentle and humble in heart, and you will find rest for your souls. For my yoke is easy and my burden is light. (Matthew 11:28–30)

Our salvation is connected with Jesus' humility, as he fulfills the Father's plan. We witness a final testimony of his humility when we gaze on his crucified body hanging on the cross, taken down, and put into the tomb.

Faith Formation

Birth and new beginnings offer parish ministers opportunities to recognize the emotions that people experience on such occasions. These include pride, joy, hope, fear, and uncertainty. Anger often accompanies beginnings that are not freely chosen. It helps to identify such emotions before looking at the ministerial possibilities they offer.

A baby's birth brings a surge of love, pride, and happiness to parents and relatives. Families usually celebrate a child's birth with gifts and congratulatory wishes. Newborn children bring anticipation to parents, who wonder what their child might become. The following story indicates the emotions to keep in mind when dealing with couples before the birth of a child.

> Jill and Sean are apprehensive as they await the birth of their first child. They hope it will be a healthy child. They worry about raising their child in an uncertain, violent world. Sean is concerned about providing adequate financial support for the family. Uncertainty accompanies their mixed emotions.

Responsible parents wonder about their children's future. Often these concerns relate to their material future, not to their responsibility to pass on the Catholic faith. The spiritual and material well-being of children triggers issues that parish ministers need to consider. They can include such matters in homilies, marriage preparation, and faith formation sessions.

New beginnings like going to college also trigger deep emotions. Pride and enthusiasm filled Sarah's heart when she left for college. She was the first in her family to pursue higher education. Her roommate, Kim, came from three generations of college graduates, so her feelings were different. Sarah and Kim hoped to meet their family's expectations as they coped with their growth into maturity. Like many first-year students,

- their emotions were not fully integrated into their personality;
- they left home for the first time;
- they now experienced freedom, but youthful enthusiasm sometimes got in the way;
- challenges presented themselves to develop bad habits, like drinking, failing to study, or skipping class;
- they felt insecure, even though they didn't show it;
- positive emotions outweighed negative ones and thrusted them forward, as they began college life and anticipated their future after graduation.

People experience emotional reactions at new beginnings, like moving on after a divorce. This is seen in Lucy's case.

> Lucy divorced her husband after he left her for a younger woman. Feeling betrayed and abandoned, Lucy initially experienced fear, anger, and doubted herself. She rarely left her apartment except for work. She said, "My divorce was like death, without a funeral, sympathy cards, flowers, or casseroles. I felt a sense of failure, betrayal, and humiliation."
>
> For a while, Lucy regarded herself as a victim and stopped attending church. Depression accompanied her uncertainty, and she found it hard to be hopeful. With little joy or enthusiasm, she felt like a failure.

Many persons are like Lucy. Pastoral ministers need to recognize their emotional state, support them, and show concern. Feeling that someone cares is often the first step toward healing.

New beginnings take many different forms. Moving on and beginning anew after a job change is one of them. The following stories indicate this point.

> After Ray's company closed, he, Marge, his wife, and Rebecca, their teenage daughter relocated in Kansas. Before that time, they had never been away from Ohio except for vacations. The new beginnings of this family were difficult, but things soon changed. They found a nice home and their neighbors welcomed them. They became involved in the local parish, and Ray enjoyed his work, which provided the family solid financial support. Contrast their story with that of Jason, Marci, and their children, ages six, ten, and sixteen.

> Jason accepted a promotion requiring the family to relocate from Texas to New York City. Abby, the el-

> dest daughter, resisted. She had two more years in high school and didn't want to leave her friends. She was a popular honor student with good possibilities for a college scholarship.
>
> Jason took the new job nonetheless. The lure of big money and his wife's encouragement persuaded him to go. After they moved, the family bought a home in a suburban neighborhood. Initially, the children thought their new house was great. Each had a private room, a luxury they did not enjoy in Texas. Soon, however, they felt the loss of their simpler ways. They experienced strong pressures to conform to the upscale lifestyle in their private school surroundings. Their class work suffered. Filled with emotions ranging from loss to anger, they struggled academically. Abby had an especially rough time. Her resentment boiled over into rebellion, and she put little effort into her schoolwork.

This family's new beginnings were not rewarding. In retrospect, Jason's family would have fared better if he refused the job offer.

The persons in the above stories experienced emotions that ranged from joy to anger and fear. Pastoral ministers perform a service when they minister with a service-oriented attitude to such people.

New beginnings are important moments in the ongoing process of Christian conversion, each representing a dying and rising. Remembering this, we can better connect the blessings and difficulties of new beginnings with those of Jesus. Those moving to a new location can unite their changes to Jesus' feelings, as he left home to begin public life. Those who suffer personal loss can connect their grieving with Mary's during the agony on the cross. Jesus' new beginnings, no matter how hard they were, led to his resurrection and return to his Father. From a faith perspective, when we wisely discern new beginnings or accept those foisted upon us, God blesses us.

We come into contact daily with people who face new beginnings.

Although some new beginnings are more significant than others, each one affords pastoral ministers a chance to minister to those undergoing such changes. They need to be particularly sensitive to people facing new beginnings, like experiencing a loss or receiving good news. When parish ministers are sensitive to those facing new beginnings, their ministry connects with people's experience and provides the driving force to witness Jesus' good news. In this regard, sacramental rites of passage are central to faith formation.

Christian Sacramental Rites of Passage

Two sacramental rites of passage, baptism and marriage, are important ways to celebrate new life. They offer wonderful opportunities for pastoral ministers to reach out to those present for the celebrations.

Baptism

Scholastic theology emphasizes that *grace builds upon nature*. This means that grace works through God's creation and elevates us from a natural to a supernatural state. God is manifested through the beauty of a sunset and the power of an ocean. Divine grace comes through nature and God's many gifts. In particular, grace accompanies human birth and new beginnings.

We situate baptism in the context of God's grace. It builds on the dynamics operative in birth itself. Birth gives life; baptism gives new life in Christ. As birth initiates us into human life, baptism initiates us into the life of Christ and the church's life.

What Jesus called *being born again* is the most fundamental change possible for humans. The new life associated with baptism centers on Jesus' death and resurrection. The Rite of Baptism for children says, "May all who are buried with Christ in the death of baptism rise also with him to the newness of life" (#54). Baptism is the most profound beginning possible for humans, for it initiates us into a new relationship with the Trinity through the church. It signals death to sin and new birth in the Spirit. Through baptism, we pass from the old way of sin to the newness of Christ's life. This gift of the Father promises new life to the one being baptized, as reflected in the following story.

New beginnings accompany life changes and offer opportunities to share Jesus' "good news."

> With an appointment at noon, I was getting ready to leave home when the phone rang at 10:27 AM. My first reaction was to let it ring, but something deep within me drew me to pick it up. The woman on the line asked frantically, "Are you a Catholic priest?" After I replied in the affirmative, she continued, "You don't know me, but I just got your name. I'm Beth, the Protestant chaplain at General Hospital in the neo-natal division. In forty minutes a small baby from a Catholic family is undergoing emergency surgery to repair his heart valve. The surgery is very risky, and the parents want the child anointed. Will you come immediately? We didn't know anyone else to call."
>
> I had never been to this hospital's neo-natal division. The surgery was to begin in less than an hour, and I did not know where to go. Besides, I had an

important meeting downtown. Before I asked why they wanted this baby anointed, the chaplain said again, "Please come, the baby weighs only about one pound."

I left the rectory and rushed to the hospital. When I arrived, I met the grateful mother. Her face showed concern for the child. I felt she desperately sought God's grace for this baby. I asked who had baptized the infant. She looked puzzled and said, "My son's never been baptized. I didn't give it a thought. I just felt he needed to be anointed to get strength." I told her that the baby should be baptized. This would make him a special child of God. It would prepare him for surgery. Relieved, she asked me to baptize him and name him John.

The hospital chaplain prepared water and brought other items for the baptism. I had never seen such a small child. John easily fit into his mother's hand with room to spare. She held him in the palm of her hand as I poured the water, said the words, and baptized him *John*.

Rarely have I seen such an outpouring of love as occurred in that neo-natal room before they took John for surgery. It was as if time stood still and the overpowering sacredness of this child's young life filled the room with emotion. The pastoral ministers were great, showing authentic Christian concern and support. The care of his mother, nurses, and staff paled in comparison to the tremendous feeling of the infinite value of John's life. That morning, he was reborn as a child of God in baptism before the doctors worked to save his life.

As the nurse wheeled baby John's cart into surgery, joy filled our hearts and tears poured from our

> eyes. At that moment the words of the *Rite of Baptism for Children* had special significance. Here we read, "God the Father of Our Lord Jesus Christ has freed you from sin, given you a new birth by water and the Holy Spirit, and welcomed you into his holy people" (#98).
>
> Slowly and meditatively, I left the hospital and drove to the meeting downtown. I don't remember what happened there but will never forget the day that God jolted me into a deeper appreciation of the sacredness of birth with that desperate telephone call. Three days later, I received another phone call from the hospital chaplain. She thanked me again and said how everyone appreciated my coming to the hospital on such short notice and baptizing John. Then, she said what I hoped to hear. The surgery was successful and they expected a full recovery. Baby John, the tiny infant, no bigger than my hand, was recovering well. In a short time, he would go home and begin a normal life with his family.

Most people celebrate a child's birth with fanfare. This joyful reaction to new life is natural. Often, baby showers precede a child's birth. Afterward, parents celebrate with parties and show off the baby to proud relatives and friends. The child receives gifts, congratulatory cards, and baby items. In such cases, we also hope that there is a spiritual dimension that was evident in the hospital room with baby John. Did I feel it because baby John was baptized or because this child's birth was a sacred event? Both were involved, but I experienced the sacredness of his life even before I baptized him. There is no doubt, however, that his baptism brought to a new level the sacredness already there. Through baptism, John was born again into the life of Christ. It brought to fruition the sacredness of his life present from birth.

> The sacredness of a child's life is diminished by society.

Birth is commercialized into an opportunity to make money through the sale of baby products. The horrible practice of abortion grounds a materialistic attitude that minimizes life's dignity. Society's pragmatism and individualism challenge life's sacred nature. When celebrating an infant's birth in secular ways, it's easy to neglect the baby's spiritual nature that gives life its ultimate meaning. Christians need to ask themselves how the cheapening of life affects them and how they celebrate the birth of their loved ones.

The implications for Christians are profound. The responsibilities for pastoral ministers are also telling. They have to assume a countercultural response to the secularization of birth and the cheapening of life, for secularism reaches subtly and deeply into the souls of Christians and parishes. Often, this happens without conscious realization: it seems natural to celebrate everything with money and material gifts.

Today's Catholics need spiritual assistance, for many have only a rudimentary knowledge of their faith.

- They may not have been schooled at home in spiritual values through religious instruction or family prayer.
- Often, the television and the Internet are their classrooms.
- They rarely hear about life's sacredness. If they do not begin here, how can they appreciate being born again as a child of God in baptism?

What can parish ministers do to help parents appreciate birth's sacredness? It means preparing parents to appreciate their child from a faith perspective. This includes creating a parish atmosphere that identifies, welcomes, and celebrates newborn children. This involves more than baptizing them. The following suggestions can enhance a parish's ministry to parents of newborn children.

- Identify pregnant parents and send spiritual cards and other materials to congratulate and prepare them spiritually for their child's birth.
- Publish the names of newborn children in parish bulletins and introduce them at Mass.
- Offer sessions for pregnant spouses, inviting them to meet other parents in like circumstances.
- Arrange gatherings for newborn moms and dads.
- Send congratulation cards to parents of newborn children, welcoming the child into the parish and providing information about baptism, catechesis, and other opportunities for newborn children and their parents.

Taking a new look may mean reviving old traditions. When I was a boy, Mom brought me to church shortly after my birth for a religious rite of passage. This involved having me blessed and *churched*. This custom, reminiscent of bringing Jesus to the temple shortly after his birth, has disappeared today. This rite centered on life itself.

Parishes can revitalize this rite in a new format. It can be celebrated soon after a baby's birth and followed not long afterward by baptism. The process can begin with general catechesis before baptism. If a parish is in contact with pregnant couples before their child's birth, it can catechize them at this time and follow up with more extensive catechesis after the baby's birth.

Birth is a key transition time that brings Catholics to fuller appreciation of faith and a deeper realization of the spiritual implications of giving birth. To revitalize the Christian faith it is important to start at the beginning, so as to set a firm foundation for subsequent growth. What better way to begin than to instill solid

Christian values into parents? We learn much by probing more deeply into the key moment of baptism. In so doing, we look to adult and infant baptism.

Adult Baptism

At the Easter Vigil, the newly initiated reflect an enthusiasm that hints of the new life of Christ's followers after Pentecost. Many Catholics participating in this celebration recognize it as the most powerful liturgical event of the year. Here, catechumens complete their initiation through the celebration of Baptism, Confirmation, and the Eucharist.

> All the church's catechetical documents since Vatican II emphasize the primacy of adult catechesis.

The Catholic community appreciates the new beginnings made possible through the RCIA for renewing the faith community. This is evident in parishes that enthusiastically enter into the process of Christian initiation of adults. As various steps and stages of the rite help catechumens and candidates grow in faith, they also renew the larger church family. The strong witness given in this process shows that new beginnings are occasions for personal and communal renewal. This realization is imperative, as growing numbers of Catholics leave the church and join evangelical megachurches or drop out completely.

Jake and Esther were interested in joining the Catholic Church. Their stories shed light on how the parish's ministry influences an adult catechumen who goes through the RCIA.

> Jake's parish put minimal efforts into the RCIA. He enrolled as a catechumen, but the rituals surrounding his formation were uninspiring. The rites reflected a parish that was going through the motions.

> Parishioners made little effort to welcome him and connect with him. Jake attended most sessions, became a member of the elect, and was baptized at the Easter Vigil. After that, he never went to a mystagogical session. He attended Mass sporadically for a year then stopped coming. Now, he is active in another Christian church.
>
> Esther, on the other hand, received a first-class initiation in her parish. The pastor and pastoral staff warmly welcomed her. She became acquainted with other parish members through invitations to attend parish functions. The community reinforced the new beginning that Esther made when she entered the catechumenate. Her family actively participated in her Christian initiation at the Easter Vigil. Two of her children entered the catechumenate the following year.

The liturgical rites that helped Esther move through the stages of the RCIA were powerful. Her father, a Lutheran, attended the Sunday liturgies at her parish when Esther participated in the scrutinies. He was uplifted as the congregation reflected on life's meaning through music, homily, and ceremonial rituals. At the conclusion of Mass, those initiated stood in the back of church and were warmly greeted by the congregation before going downstairs for hospitality.

Jake's parish never appreciated the power of the RCIA to bring about new beginnings in the faith journey of the catechumens, candidates, and community. As a result, nothing much happened. The graces of the Holy Spirit did not flow as fully as they did in Esther's case. His parish was not as strong a channel for these graces as was the community that welcomed Esther.

The RCIA contains dynamics that can be applied during any new beginning. We need to hear God's Word again and again from welcoming, interested Christians. If we do not reflect Jesus' good news in our neighborhood, workplace, or family, who will? How can God's Word be enfleshed except through us? Parish ministers must take the lead in recognizing the significance of adult faith formation and focus on it in renewing the entire parish.

Infant Baptism

Mary, a volunteer, frustrated at her parish's lack of interest in finding new ways to minister effectively, said, "I don't get it. Catholics in this parish walk out the door and don't return. Music is drab, homilies are uninspiring, and ministry doesn't seem effective. Maybe I'm missing something, but let me tell you about my son, Aaron."

> "Aaron," Mary said, "is twenty-seven, married to Beth, a Methodist. Neither is active in their faith. When married three years ago, their preparation was minimal. They filled out the required forms, spoke to a marriage minister, did a FOCCUS inventory, and attended a one-day pre-Cana conference. They fulfilled the necessary requirements to get married in the Catholic Church. The marriage minister was nice, but seemed tired.
>
> "Aaron and Beth said little about their preparation, but I got the impression that it didn't inspire them. After the wedding, they rarely attended church. After their first child, Kirby, was born, they wondered about his baptism. Unsure of what to do and feeling pressure from me, they went to the parish to ask about his baptism. The parish minister asked whether they were active Catholics. They replied honestly. Aaron indicated his willingness to come to Mass regularly and raise Kirby as a Catholic. The baby was baptized.

> "I predict that Aaron will stop attending church and Kirby will receive little or no formation in prayer or Catholic teaching. The next time religion may arise is when Kirby goes to school or is old enough to make his First Communion.
>
> "The parish ministers missed two great opportunities to refocus Aaron's faith, speak to Beth about her beliefs, and lead them on the path of an ecumenical Christian family. My son's experience is not unique. While some parishes are *busy about many things*, they often neglect what is most basic—to minister to people when they are in need."

Mary said it well. Catholic parishes and pastoral ministers need to regularly examine how they minister to families when a baby is baptized. Many Catholic parents are ignorant of basic church teaching. They may not raise their children as Catholics because faith is not a priority. Others do not know what to teach their children about God or the church, because they never learned basic Catholic beliefs and practices.

Without a strong focus on faith how can we expect the vitality of Catholic parishes to continue? Jesus said that if we build a foundation on sand it will collapse. We must build the parish's future on well-formed parents who catechize their children.

Baptism is a key moment for conversion. How blessed are parents if pastoral ministers realize this and help parents see that the joy at their child's birth is fulfilled in the new life that baptism brings! Today, this is happening in many Catholic parishes. Where it happens, parish ministers often make people feel welcome, catechize them, offer counseling, introduce them to other parents who have children baptized about the same time, and provide concrete ways to continue their faith formation. Ministerial leaders invite interested adults to various forms of volunteer ministry, so that baptism becomes a powerful moment for parishes to celebrate, and a new step along the faith path of parents.

Another basic Christian rite of passage takes place as a couple marries. Ministry at this time is of special significance for parish ministers.

Marriage

The sacrament of Matrimony serves the larger community through the love of a man and woman. The fruit of their love is a child: their love continues the human race. Marriage primarily is intended for others, not selfishly for the couple alone.

God's love is reflected powerfully in the love of husband and wife. In giving of themselves, they experience a foretaste of God's love, a love they share with each other and their children. The Nuptial Blessing in the *Rite for Marriage* says, "Father, to reveal the plan of your love, you made the union of husband and wife an image of the covenant between you and your people" (#120). Rooted in love, marriage is a key time for a man and a woman. It is important that family members, friends, and church ministers recognize marriage as such and treat couples accordingly.

When a couple looks toward marriage, they plan to end one lifestyle and begin another. One early consideration is where they wish to be married. If both parties are Catholic or one is Catholic and the other is not Catholic, they usually get married in the Catholic parish. Catholics irregular in the practice of their faith may not know what is involved or where to begin. At this time, many are open to looking anew at their faith. Whether or not marriage provides an occasion for growth in faith often depends on how a parish's personnel, including secretaries, treat them, when they inquire about getting married.

- It's unfortunate when a couple to be married is asked initially by a pastoral minister, "Do you regularly go to church here or use the envelopes," as a condition for celebrating their marriage in the parish. Such a cold, matter-of-fact response turns off couples and causes some to leave the church.

- Marriage is a fruitful time for pastoral ministers to be positive and help a couple see God's role in their marriage and to connect them with the church. Couples know right away whether they are welcome or not. It is the starting point that can bring them into active participation with the parish community.

- Marriage is a significant milestone on a couple's faith journey. Sensitive pastoral ministers assist them as they form positive attitudes, grow in faith, and learn to pray as a couple.

Parish ministers are given a great opportunity to shift the thinking of a couple from a casual to a more serious regard for spiritual matters as they prepare for marriage.

Pastoral ministers are privileged to prepare couples well for this wonderful event and help engaged couples feel like real members of the church, about to enter a new phase in their love for each other, neighbor, Christ, and church. Increasingly, as Catholics marry persons of other faiths, all married couples must be encouraged to regard their marriage as a holy union between themselves and God. The way they are treated often affects whether or not they stay connected with the church.

THE MAIN POINTS IN THIS CHAPTER

- Because people can see the implications of their actions, pastoral ministers can give them love, encouragement, and support during transition times, like birth, leaving for the military service, college, sickness, and death.
- Birth, a fundamental human experience, has always been surrounded by rituals, often of a religious nature.
- While some pastoral ministers do little to help parishioners appreciate the spiritual implications of birth, secular advertisers make the most of it for monetary gain. Pastoral ministers can learn from this business approach to acknowledge a child's birth as a special time to encourage new church membership and show parents that the parish too celebrates their child's birth.
- Challenges always exist with new beginnings, especially if they involve separation from family and friends.
- Jesus' birth into the world places every child's birth in a new light. His birth glorified the miracle of birth and invites parents to see their child's birth as an unmatched spiritual event.
- The paradox of our salvation is connected with Jesus' humility as he fulfills the Father's plan without fanfare or demanding anything but love.
- Birth and new beginnings offer parish ministers opportunities to recognize the emotions that people typically experience on such occasions. People in every community face new beginnings daily which represent a dying and rising and are important moments in the ongoing process of Christian conversion.

- Vibrant parishes, especially their leaders, need to be particularly sensitive to people facing new beginnings, like experiencing a loss or receiving good news, so that their ministry connects with people's experiences and provides the driving force to witness Jesus' good news.
- Birth gives life, baptism gives new life in Christ; birth initiates us into human life, baptism initiates us into the church's life.
- The sacredness of a child's life is diminished by society, as birth is commercialized. Pastoral ministers need to take a new look at birth as a spiritual event and ask what they can do to help parents appreciate birth's sacredness. Pastoral ministers must assume a countercultural response to the secularization of birth and the cheapening of life.
- The Catholic community, especially parish ministers, need to appreciate the new beginnings made possible through the RCIA for renewing the faith community. They also need to examine how they minister to families when a baby is baptized.
- It is a real blessing when pastoral ministers focus on baptism as a key moment for conversion and help parents see that the joy at their child's birth is fulfilled in the new life that baptism brings.
- Since marriage is a significant milestone on a couple's faith journey, pastoral ministers can assist them as they form positive attitudes, grow in faith, and learn to pray together.

As a group talk about this chapter, using these questions:

- Reflect upon three transition times, key moments, or rites of passage in your life. Why were they important and what consequences came from them? During these times, how did the Catholic community support you?

- Reflect on the significance of new births in your life or family. To what degree are they regarded as sacred or secular events? Discuss how you can use them as occasions for probing more deeply into the mystery of God's love.
- Identify three new beginnings in your life or the life of someone you love. Did they involve a rite of passage? To what degree did you or those involved see them as opportunities to bring faith and Christian concern to those involved? Discuss several opportunities that you or your parish took advantage of or missed.
- Discuss Jesus' birth and new beginnings as adding fresh insights to real life experiences that happened to you or someone you know.
- How do you see birth and new beginnings as occasions for faith formation? What stories from your life indicate the power of birth or new beginnings in faith formation?
- If you were asked to develop a process to help your parish better respond to births and new beginnings in parishioners' lives, how would you begin and what would you include?
- Reflect on the connection between community, faith formation, and the sacrament of marriage. Apply your conclusions to your life.

This chapter has considered new beginnings. They bring about changes and opportunities for growth, which Chapter Six considers.

CHAPTER SIX

Life Changes and Growth

This chapter considers life experiences associated with change and growth.

We begin taking a deeper look by

- telling the story of the beautiful lake;
- considering growth, change, and rites of passage, which help people adjust and move on. Such times provide Christians the opportunity to share Jesus' love;
- reflecting on Jesus as our model to imitate;
- seeing change and growth as opportunities for faith formation.

Next, we examine the main points in this chapter. Finally, we offer some discussion questions.

Take a Deeper Look

Two bulldozers churned deeper into the once pristine farm field. Oozing mud and sludge from a recent rain replaced the golden sheaves of wheat that had proudly ascended heavenward. The field changed appearance, because I hoped to solve the erosion problem that turned the center part of this hay field into a swamp each spring and fall.

When the bulldozers did their work, everything became drab and depressing. The field was totally wasted, except for limestone and clay that protruded from its surface at the bottom of the seventeen foot basin. Hour after hour, the bulldozers pushed dirt from the center to one side, fashioning a dam about three hundred feet long, twenty-two feet deep, and wide enough to construct a road across its top.

Gradually, the bulldozers finished their work. I stood by the side of the new lake and gazed at a deep hole, which I hoped would fill up and become a one and one-quarter acre lake. When the contour of the ground remained the same for three months, I thought the lake might never fill.

By the second year grass, weeds, and briar bushes covered the bare dirt around the water. Then, I saw the first bird land on the water of this rapidly developing pristine lake, anchored in the center by a living spring. Over the next five years, I planted white pine trees around the lake. Nature took care of the rest, as black locust, sycamore, and tulip poplar trees formed a canopy around it. After they matured, what lay beyond the lake was no longer visible from the road.

As the natural landscape changed, deer, crickets, turkeys, frogs, and turtles made the area their home. Before my eyes, I experienced a beautiful transformation, never anticipated when beginning this venture. It's hard to fathom that from a sloppy mess of swampland thirty-five years ago, it became a beautiful spot, home to various species of vegetation and animals that inhabit this part of Indiana. Today, the lake contains a fine living balance of plants, animals, trees, flowers, and weeds.

When standing near the lake, I feel like a visitor on the land. This is God's land, home to the animals, trees, plants, friends, and me. As I reflect on the marvel of nature that developed over these years, I appreciate more the profound mystery of change and growth, both necessary aspects of life. During the many years I visited this place, I witnessed my own growth and that of my neighbors, family, friends, and parents. As Ecclesiastes says,

> What do people gain from all the toil at which they toil under the sun? A generation goes, a generation comes, but the earth remains forever....What has been is what will be, and what has been done is what will be done; there is nothing new under the sun. (1:3–4, 9)

Like the land, my mother, father, sisters, brother, and I changed. Dad died first and Mom lived many more years to enjoy the land with our family. Growth and change are inevitable parts of life and offer us opportunities to reach our potential and prepare for eternal life. They also offer pastoral ministers a fertile ground for ministry in Jesus' name.

Life Moments: Change and Growth

The rebirth of the land after the lake's construction serves as a jumping off point to consider human change and growth. Before I built the lake, anxiety, concern, and fear made me wonder if I was doing the right thing. Similar emotions exist with other life changes. This is especially true during transition times, like a paralyzing sickness or moving to a new city, often accompanied by significant emotional baggage. Individuals, family members, friends, and pastoral ministers need to recognize such emotions.

Change and growth happen in steady, yet unpredictable ways. Joys, celebrations, and roadblocks sometimes interrupt growth. The general tone established in the church's liturgical year follows life's changing patterns. Special times and feasts are interspersed during the regular course of the year. The liturgical year focuses on the two dynamics of ordinary and special times. The expression "Ordinary Time" reminds us that we work out our salvation in the flesh and blood experiences of ordinary life. This is reflected in Elizabeth and Sally's stories.

> Elizabeth, an elderly widow, entered a senior care facility. Five years before, she had taken care of her sickly husband prior to his death. As a mother, she raised a large family. Never concerned about herself, Elizabeth heard Jesus' words about loving neighbor as one loves oneself.
>
> Sally, a former member of a religious community, left the convent while a missionary in Brazil. She stayed there and ministered to the poor on the streets of a small village. Few outside her area knew her name. That meant little to her. She knew that God works in life's ordinary events.

People like Elizabeth and Sally look to Jesus as their model—as they witness Jesus' presence in ordinary events, sometimes with neglected or sick people—as they go about their daily duties. Like Jesus, they respond to a beggar, a hurting woman, or a sick child. His birth, suffering, and death inspire them. From Jesus they get the courage to respond to life's sacrifices, dyings, and risings.

A success-oriented culture looks for spectacular events and can easily miss God's presence in the ordinary. Many parents push their children too hard to excel in sports, academic work, or other activities. In this culture, pastoral ministers can ask,

- Does pushing children into multiple activities help them develop solid values and healthy attitudes?
- How can parents focus on nurturing balanced children, growing out of ordinary experiences?
- How can pastoral ministers encourage parents to bring a sense of balance into children's activities?

Keeping children busy in various activities doesn't necessarily create a good self-image in them. The focus needs to be on raising balanced children with good self images and helping them sort out their priorities. Developing a positive image is connected with seeing oneself as God sees us. Pastoral ministers can help them do this. The saints did ordinary things in a faith-filled way. This is greatness. A profound awe often comes over us as we hear stories of ordinary people who lived in extraordinary ways. Such awe centers on those who accepted life's joys and trials with faith. Most lived simply, caring for others and serving God, family, and neighbor.

Developing solid human values begins in infancy and lasts a lifetime. As I reflect on the slow, steady process involved, I recall what happened during the construction of the lake. Beforehand, various plants, weeds, trees, deer, birds, rocks, and other local inhabitants lived in the way that nature designated in swampy land. From an ecological viewpoint, life was well balanced there with circumstances changing little from year to year. Its ordinariness came from its balanced natural patterns. When the bulldozers came, the landscape changed. Altering the soil configuration unleashed new dynamics on the earth. Old ways died and new birth happened. This occurred because plants and animals possess a built-in ability to adapt to new surroundings. New species entered the arena, made possible because of a better balance of sun, earth, and water.

Watching the landscape's changing panorama, I realized that like the plants and animals around the lake, humans too develop value systems during ordinary times. When nurturing faith in the crucible of ordinary life, we develop values into strengths that enable us to adapt during traumatic events, like sickness or death. Solidly based in life, such times enable us to reach new plateaus of growth and holiness.

What happened to the land over forty years is a mirror image of what occurs when solid values learned in ordinary time enable us to cope with new challenges. The dyings and risings, reflected through nature and illustrated in the story of the lake, are central to growth and maturity. When pastoral ministers make little progress, remember that God's timing is not our timing. Often, the values a minister conveys take years to bear fruit.

Change, though inevitable and sometimes scary, provides an occasion for a new beginning. An ending is always the beginning of something new, as we learn from Jesus, our model.

Jesus as Model

Homilists, biblical scholars, pastoral ministers, and theologians remind us that Jesus was like us in all things, except sin.

- His lifestyle mirrored his age and maturity.
- Jesus, a good Jew, was faithful to the Torah and remarkable in his ordinariness.
- When he entered the synagogue at Nazareth and read from the Torah, those present recognized him as Joseph's son (Luke 4:16–21).
- When Jesus applied Isaiah's words to himself, he identified himself with the Messiah who was to come.
- Those present refused to accept his words, cast him from the synagogue, and dragged him from town.

When Jesus' mission began, his lifestyle shifted, and the royal road to the cross was irretrievably set. From this point on, Jesus set out to fulfill the mission that his Father gave him. This accomplished, he said, "Father, into your hands I commend my spirit." Then he died (Luke 23:46).

Jesus' willingness to fulfill his mission gives pastoral ministers courage, as their responsibilities change. He never shirked his responsibilities at any stage of his ministry or during his passion and death. Although our mission is different from his, we need to accept the changes that come our way. We get divine help to do so by acting courageously as Jesus did, thus imitating Jesus' virtues of courage and perseverance.

Courage

Jesus was a young man still learning the ways of Jewish law when he stood up in the synagogue, interpreted the Torah, and applied the words of Isaiah to himself. He refused to give in to the opposition of synagogue elders, rabbis, and friends. Later in his ministry he remained firm, even when threatened by death. He shows courage in this passage from John:

> Pilate therefore said to him, "Do you refuse to speak to me? Do you not know that I have power to release you, and power to crucify you?" Jesus answered him, "You would have no power over me unless it had been given you from above…." (John 19:10–11)

During this encounter, Mary saw Jesus' courage. Did she then picture Jesus' ultimate fate? Did she recall the temple episode when Jesus stayed behind and spoke with the learned men? Then he talked with the leaders, now he challenges them. In both cases, Jesus remained strong. Did Mary recall the devil's temptation of Jesus in the desert or the Scribes and Pharisees opposing him for curing on the Sabbath? Did she remember when he preached to the five thousand?

Picture Mary's amazement at Jesus' courage, when he hung dying on the cross. Did his courage help to sustain her? She gave him life and modeled courage at his birth, during the flight into Egypt, and the family's return to Nazareth. On Calvary, Jesus showed her the courage that epitomized his total self-surrender to God. Seeing present difficulties through Mary's eyes strengthens pastoral ministers, as they help hurting people, as indicated in Edwin's story.

> Edwin, a man in his thirties, waits patiently as his critically ill wife fights for her life in the hospital. This is the third time she has been there during the past year. Their youngest daughter suffers from a rare blood ailment. The toll on him has been tremendous. Yet, God's grace sustains his courage, seen in the unselfish way he balances work and family responsibilities. Courage like his can come only from God. And it did not come overnight.

For years, Edwin prayed, attended Mass, received the sacraments, read the Scriptures, and taught his family to love God and serve others. His faith prepared him for the present challenge. It taught him that when human energy wanes, and friends, doctors, and family can do no more than support him, the courage to go on must come from God. He roots his courage in faith, not words.

Something similar can be said of pastoral ministers who become tired, disappointed, and weary because everything is going wrong. At such times, they need to remember that God, not they, decides the final course of things. Courage enables them to go on, in spite of difficulties.

Remembering Jesus' courage gives hope and as we strive to imitate Jesus, we learn more about perseverance.

Perseverance

During life's changes, we need courage to continue on life's path.

Margaret, a Christian native woman belongs to the turtle clan. When she was discussing her spirituality with a Hispanic friend, José, he asked whether belonging to the turtle clan influenced it. Surprised at the question, she looked at him as if to say, "You don't get it." Seeing her reaction, José asked,

> "Margaret, why did your facial expression change when I asked you this question?" She replied, "Since I belong to the turtle clan, the turtle's spirit *is the foundation* of my spirituality. My native spirituality is the foundation for my personal spirituality and my Christian spirituality. The Father, Son, and Holy Spirit speak to me through my roots as a turtle clan member. These native roots remind me who I am."
>
> "How does this make a practical difference?"
>
> "You know how I operate. You also realize from your experiences in the woods how turtles act. You've seen both of us in action. How does a turtle act? How does it move? It moves cautiously and slowly, as I do. If danger lurks in the vicinity, it curls into its shell to protect itself; so do I. If a barrier is put in a turtle's way, it goes around or over it. If it cannot, it dies trying. So do I. I recognize the Spirit's action in the world through such eyes, as you see your life through the lens that formed you. The turtle's spirit and mine have become one. From my Christian faith, I know both are rooted in the Word of God and the creator's activity. God gives me my natural life and blesses me with new life in Jesus."

The turtle's perseverance in getting over or around obstacles mirrors Margaret's. Jesus' perseverance, seen through the turtle's spirit, invites her to see her experiences in light of Jesus' perseverance. When religious leaders opposed him and some disciples left after he promised to give them his flesh and blood to eat and drink, Jesus remained true to his mission. After most of his followers abandoned him on the cross, Jesus persevered. He didn't walk away from the obstacles in the way of accomplishing his mission. Neither does Margaret.

Jesus endured the agony of the cross to win our salvation. Imitating his perseverance, pastoral ministers, and Christians generally, can overcome the obstacles in their path. They can persevere, just as Mary did through the strength given her by her son.

Faith Formation

> When teaching high school juniors, Ed realized that the grades of some students who did well in their first two years dropped appreciably in their third year. At first, he attributed it to their getting part-time jobs. Then, he realized that many of them got driver's licenses over the summer. It was after that that things changed. While not true of all students, the trend was important enough to let Ed see that getting a driver's license is a significant time for young people. For many, it is the most important rite of passage in their teenage years.

Pastoral ministers need to recognize such transition times as ministerial opportunities and react positively to them. They can anticipate some transition times, like getting a driver's license or graduating from high school. Others—like changing careers because of a work-related accident or switching colleges because of new family responsibilities—they cannot. Such awareness precedes effective faith formation, for each life transition offers an entry point for ministry. Occasions like this may help people turn to Jesus, deepen their faith, or begin new church association. The first step to maximizing the opportunities that life transitions afford is to identify them. Only then can we decide how to respond. Some life transitions include:

- beginning kindergarten and the first grade;
- graduating from the eighth grade;
- winning a championship;
- receiving an art award;
- getting a driver's license;
- graduating from high school;
- earning a college scholarship;
- getting a divorce;
- receiving a promotion at work;
- receiving a citation for excellent teaching in a classroom;
- having a miscarriage;
- accepting new leadership responsibilities;
- retiring from a job;
- becoming seriously ill or dying.

Such times are opportunities for pastoral ministers to connect with people when they are more open to faith. Since they offer entry points for ministry, ministers need to recognize them to be more effective.

Getting a Driver's License

When speaking about rites of passage to parents or high school catechists, I ask, "What is the most important event in a teenager's life?" Usually, the immediate response is, "Getting their driver's license!" I continue, "How many of your parishes have a ritual celebrating this event?" Rarely, does anyone say that they ritualize it. Rather, the room grows silent. I inquire, "Why not?" Again, there is silence.

The Christian community needs to help teenagers spiritually at times like getting a driver's license.

The material side of learning to drive takes care of itself. To celebrate it, some parents buy their son or daughter a new car or give them use of the family's automobile. But how do they instill the importance of deeper values, like being responsible with the car or acting properly when driving? Parents, pastoral ministers, and teachers are encouraged to establish a ritual or rite of passage to help teenagers accept their responsibilities. Below are points for consideration.

- Gather six or eight parents, parish ministers, and teenagers to consider this issue. The initial work may begin at least one year before getting a license.
- Set general directions for a culminating ritual, when car keys are turned over to teenagers, and, in turn, they sign a covenant of responsibility. Will the ritual happen in church or a special place? Will it be a group or individual event? What will be involved in the ritual? Will it be mandatory before getting permission to drive?
- Consider elements in the ritual, like: the criteria for getting and keeping the car keys, a contract signed by parents and teenagers during the ritual, an actual handing over of the keys and signing the contract, a sacred symbol to put in the car, like a crucifix or St. Christopher medal, and an agreement to return the keys if the contract is violated.
- Include sessions for the parents and teenagers to discuss

> the responsibilities of teenagers, relationships with their parents, how to act in the car and with the car, prayer before driving, and the culminating ritual.

A ritual like this depends on the creativity and commitment of parents and parish ministers. Since parents are concerned about their teenager's well-being when driving, many are open to participate in such a ritual to assist their sons or daughters.

Graduating from High School

After graduation from high school, young adults head for college, military service, or employment. They need advice, direction, and continued contact with the Christian community. During the period, from age eighteen until they marry, young adults often lose contact with their parish. Some consider this the least spiritual time in their lives. Students entering college often get little help in adjusting to their new lifestyle. This is illustrated in Chuck's story.

> Chuck lived with his divorced mother and sister until he graduated from South Central High. During his senior year, he could not wait to leave home. After graduation, he chose a college several hundred miles away. When he arrived, he felt lost. He had great fun meeting new friends, but it wasn't the same as at home. At night, he returned to a cold dorm. No one did his laundry or got him meals. There was no refrigerator to raid if he was hungry at night. He ate in a cafeteria, where everything soon tasted the same. Chuck missed his high school buddies. The new university was big, and his roommate often was drunk. He felt pressure to conform to the behavior of guys whose values were not the same as his were. He

> became depressed and it took him most of the freshman year to adjust to his surroundings.

Chuck's story is not necessarily the norm. Many college students have positive experiences, adjust smoothly, have good roommates, and like the change into college. Emily is one of them.

> The first time Emily met Ann, her roommate, they hit it off. Soon, they became best friends. They studied together and discussed their classes. When certain guys and gals pressured them to party too much, they had each other. Nonetheless, they missed their families and friends at home.

Chuck, Emily, and Ann had little contact with their home parishes after they left for college. Chuck was Methodist, and the two women were Catholic. When transitioning into college, it would have helped if they knew their parishes prayed for them and kept in contact. Pastoral ministers can take the lead to see that this happens.

Some college students go to church only when they come home for a visit to their families. While at college, many students welcome contact with their home parish. This can make the difference between staying Catholic or leaving the church. The following suggestions help students maintain such contact:

- When students graduate from high school, parish ministers can get their college e-mail addresses. Give them a sacred symbol, like a crucifix, picture, or a Bible from the parish as they leave for college and encourage them to put it in their room.
- Have a parishioner coordinate ongoing e-mail contact with all college students.
- Each week, send them a note, indicating that the parish is

praying for them. Include a short prayer they can say and a brief spiritual reflection, possibly from the Sunday Mass readings. Indicate key events going on in the parish that might interest them.

- Around Thanksgiving, send a notice about a reunion of all college students and military personnel over Christmas. Give the date and ask them to keep it open. Invite those who have time to help plan this event. Have it at the parish and tell them to bring their friends. Provide food and entertainment.

Students going to college often lose contact with their parishes, even though they may go to Mass with their families when at home.

Although Christmas is a busy time, students want to see their friends. What better place to do this than at the parish! If parishes see young adults as a priority, they take the time, expend the effort, and spend the money to make events like this happen. What is mentioned here about going to college can be applied to men and women in the military.

Assuming New Leadership Responsibilities

Leadership occurs in community affairs, work, or volunteer projects. These are accompanied by new responsibilities and pressures that affect the individual, those working with the person, and their families. Frequently, one accepts a new leadership role without thinking through the consequences. This is illustrated in the following story told by a pastoral minister.

> Gwendolyn, a nurse, was happily married with three children. For several years, she assumed more and

> more volunteer parish roles. She was president of the worship commission, a catechist, and helped at the fish fry. In addition to her full-time work in the hospital, she was at church, gone from her family, three evenings each week. Her husband did not appreciate her heavy parish involvement, but left it up to her. One evening before she left for church, her young son, Sean, became disturbed when she told him she was going to church again.
>
> During the previous week, Sean and his mom were reading fairy tales with the goal of learning good values. They discussed them after he finished each one. When he read the tale of the "Big Bad Wolf," symbolic of wrong or evil, Sean's goal was to get the Big Bad Wolf out of his life. He had a hard time figuring out what to do with him.
>
> When Gwendolyn returned home after the church meeting, Sean waited enthusiastically for her. He ran to her and said, "Mommy, you promised that we would have a party, if I got rid of the Big Bad Wolf. I did it! I got rid of him forever. Let's have the party."
>
> Curious as to what Sean did with the Big Bad Wolf, Gwendolyn said, "Sure, Sean, we'll have a party, but first tell me what you did with the Big Bad Wolf." Without smiling, and in a very somber tone he said, "I sent him to church for a meeting." Sean was serious. He associated evil with the church that took his Mom away from him.

Gwendolyn thought seriously about Sean's answer. She got the point and dropped out of most church activities until Sean was older. She saw that her first responsibility was to her family. Gwendolyn realized after hearing Sean's words that assuming more parish leadership roles were counterproductive to her family. A parish minister could have pointed this out to her, before she realized that she was neglecting her family. She could have profited from such advice.

Each new leadership role brings more responsibilities and added pressures.

Something similar can be done to help parish members facing tough choices concerning new jobs or added responsibilities. When such occasions arise, it is wise to consider how such new roles will affect the person, the family, and friends. The best choice often is not the one paying the most money.

It's easy to get a "big head" when climbing the corporate ladder. An old adage says, "Humans create structures and they in turn recreate us." People assuming new leadership roles must be careful that the roles do not recreate them into people they are not. Friends, family members, and pastoral ministers can provide a great service when individuals face a life change involving new leadership roles.

Retiring from a Job

Since retirement represents a significant change and a new beginning, many adults need help to face it. They know things will be different in retirement and wonder about the future. Parishes rarely provide assistance to help them. Healthy older adults are one group that parishes often neglect. They may be looking for more than volunteering their time and giving money. A key time for ministry is when they retire. In this context, pastoral ministers might ask:

- Does the parish have religious events for retirees?
- Do parish ministries deal with the spiritual implications of retirement?

Retirement can be a traumatic time.

- What religious literature is available? How can the parish help retired persons with responsibilities for aged parents, children, or grandchildren?
- Who talks to the elderly about sickness, death, and the afterlife?
- What else is already occurring in the parish to minister to healthy older adults?
- How can the parish better address the spiritual concerns of retired persons and those about to retire?
- What spiritual opportunities can be made available for the elderly in the form of prayer and spiritual direction?
- How can the elderly contribute to the parish?

Since retirement is a significant transition time for older adults, parish ministers and the wider parish community need to minister to them in a very positive way. The church can learn from the example of the early Christians who selected Matthias to take Judas' place (Acts 1:23–26). They also appointed seven deacons to care for widows and the aged (Acts 6:1–6). These biblical passages can be applied to caring for the elderly.

Getting a driver's license, graduating from high school, assuming a new leadership role, and retiring are four instances of important transition times. The community can establish rites of passage to ritualize them. Each can be an entry point for ministry.

Pastoral ministers need to respond with love and compassionate understanding to life transitions that families, friends, or colleagues undergo. Doing so makes the Christian message come alive and helps the parish grow. This was Jesus' way. It needs to be our way also. The sacraments of Eucharist and Confirmation help us.

Christian Sacramental Rites of Passage

First Communion

First Communion usually occurs in childhood. The following episode occurred shortly after seven-year-old Suzie received her First Communion.

> Suzie told her Mom she wanted to go to a special pizza place near her home to celebrate after her First Communion. The Friday after she received Jesus for the first time, she, her brother, younger sister, and parents went there. They sat near a window.
>
> As they began to eat, Suzie noticed a homeless man wandering into the parking lot and rooting through the dumpster for food. Visibly upset, she said, "We have to get something for that man to eat." Her Dad ordered him a hamburger and French fries. When the order arrived, Dad and Suzie brought the food to him. He graciously accepted and sat at the curb eating his treat.
>
> After they returned, Suzie's Mom said, "Suzie, tonight you were Eucharist for that man." Suzie replied, "No, Mommy. We will never be Eucharist for him until we invite him inside to eat at the table with us."

In her simple way, Suzie got the message of her First Communion. She associated receiving Jesus' body and blood under the appearances of bread and wine with responding in love to this homeless man, also a member of Christ's body. This is reflected in the *Catechism of the Catholic Church*, "…by this sacrament we unite ourselves to Christ, who makes us sharers in his Body and Blood to form a single body" (#1331).

At First Communion, pastoral ministers can minister in special ways to the communicants, parents, and families. This rite of passage implies parental responsibilities that go beyond First Communion day. It provides an occasion for pastoral ministers to help children grow in love for Jesus in the Eucharist, for parents to provide a Catholic upbringing for their children, and for the family to become an active part of the parish.

Parents are obliged to bring children to Mass every Sunday, preferring it to soccer, baseball, or dance lessons.

Many parents are open to grow in faith as they assist children spiritually, but often they don't know how. They need to be gently encouraged to see what their child's First Communion entails for them as Catholic parents.

Parents set the example themselves by going to Mass and by developing prayer patterns at home. For this to happen, adequate faith formation is necessary. The following suggestions are offered for pastoral ministers:

- Brainstorm with parish ministers, teachers, and parents about useful and creative ways to help prepare children and parents at First Communion. This includes how many times to meet and when and what to include in the meetings.
- Commit the parish to solid faith formation for the parents of first communicants in Catholic school and parish ministry programs.
- Recognize that some Catholic parents have rudimentary knowledge of the faith. Many times, they are unsure of church teachings and of different ways to pray.
- Arrange meetings to prepare parents for their child's First Communion. Include the pastor, if possible.
- Be open to meet in various parish settings, like the church, classroom, and pastoral center. At one session include a

potluck dinner, concentrating on Christian hospitality and prayer. Arrange a comfortable prayer space, making available materials for parents to take home. Give them options for praying with their family and children. Do a reflective prayer, similar to a Taizé prayer, with the group. Many parents have never experienced such prayer.

- Provide basic content materials for parents, presenting the church's teaching on Penance and Eucharist.
- Make books available for purchase to help parents learn more about their faith.
- Give parents e-mail sites with information about books that are used for children's sacramental preparation.

Confirmation

When confirmation is celebrated in junior high or high school, it offers an opportunity for pastoral ministers to help young people to begin their transition time from childhood to adulthood. As *Lumen Gentium* says, "By the sacrament of confirmation they are more perfectly bound to the Church and are endowed with the special strength of the Holy Spirit. Hence they are, as true witnesses of Christ, more strictly obliged to spread the faith by word and deed" (#11, Flannery translation).

Confirmation provides an occasion for pastoral ministers and parents to encourage teenagers to take responsibility for their actions. When Confirmation precedes getting a driver's license, preparation for it can link a teenager's responsibility when driving a car to Jesus' commandment to love God and neighbor.

God gives teenagers special help in confirmation to deal with their problems. The *Catechism* says, confirmation "...completes the grace of baptism by a special outpouring of the gifts of the Holy Spirit..." (Glossary, p. 872). This grace helps them at key times in their lives. Confirmation is a wonderful opportunity to teach young people the deeper meaning of sanctifying and actual grace. Catechists can encourage them to see that they bring God's grace to each other through kindness, forgiveness, and good example. The special outpouring of the gifts of the Holy Spirit can be linked to the ritual of giving teenagers the car keys, when they get a driver's license. In so doing, confirmation's spiritual effects connect with this important time for teenagers.

During life's transitions we need special graces. The grace received at confirmation helps us, for, like the graces of baptism, the grace of confirmation continues as life changes.

Celebrating rites of passage can revitalize a parish by supporting the Holy Spirit's action in people's lives. Such transition times need to be acted upon. Doing so is at the heart of Christian discipleship.

THE MAIN POINTS IN THIS CHAPTER

- Growth and change, inevitable parts of life, are symbolized by the story of the beautiful lake. They provide opportunities to reach our potential and prepare for eternal life. We need to remember that strong emotions accompany change and growth.
- The general tone established in the church's liturgical year follows life's changing patterns. Special times and feasts are interspersed during the regular course of the liturgical year.
- A success-oriented culture looks for spectacular events and can easily miss God's presence in the ordinary. It takes time to develop solid human values, beginning in infancy and lasting a lifetime.
- Parish ministers can help parents recognize that keeping

children busy in various activities doesn't necessarily create a good self-image in a child.

- Change, though inevitable and sometimes scary, is not the end. It provides an occasion for new beginnings. During life's changes, we often need courage to continue on life's path.
- Jesus is our model, and his willingness to fulfill his mission in the midst of difficulty gives us courage, as our responsibilities change. Jesus remained steadfast in his ministry, when threatened by suffering and death.
- Transition times involving rites of passage include: getting a driver's license, graduating from high school, accepting new leadership responsibilities, and retiring from a job. Parents, individuals, and pastoral ministers need to see these transition times as ministerial opportunities.
- The Christian community can help teenagers spiritually at times like getting a driver's license. When young adults head for college, military service, or employment, they need advice, direction, and continued contact with the Christian community.
- Pastoral ministers can provide wise advice to those assuming new leadership roles that may affect their families, faith response, attitudes, and ways of thinking.
- Since retirement is a significant transition time for older adults, pastoral ministers need to minister to them at this time. When pastoral ministers respond in love to the life transitions that families, friends, or colleagues undergo, the Christian message comes alive and helps the parish grow.
- At First Communion, pastoral ministers need to minister to the communicants, parents, and families in a special

way. Many parents are open to grow in faith as they assist children spiritually, but often, they don't know how.

- Parents are obliged to bring children to Mass every Sunday, preferring Mass to soccer, baseball, or dance lessons. Parents set the example themselves by going to Mass and by developing prayer patterns at home, but for this to happen, adequate faith formation is necessary.
- Confirmation provides an occasion to encourage teenagers to take responsibility for their actions. Celebrating this sacramental rites of passage can revitalize a parish by supporting the Holy Spirit's action in young people's lives.

As a group talk about this chapter, using these questions:

- Identify three major changes in your life. Why were they significant? What did you learn from them? Who supported you? What help did you receive from the Catholic parish?
- In what ways can you connect Jesus' life with your life changes? What specific virtues in his life do you recognize as important in your own and why? How do courage and perseverance help you go on when faced with challenges and difficulties?
- Cite instances when your faith grew as a result of rites of passage. What helped you or would have most helped you if offered by the parish or other Christians?
- After reflecting upon getting a driver's license, graduating from high school, assuming a new leadership role, and retiring, what other transition times, often involving rites of passage, must be kept in mind when you, family members, or friends experience them in the future? Why?

- Discuss confirmation as an opportunity to connect it with other rites of passage.
- How seriously do you believe that parents take their responsibilities to help their children grow in faith as they prepare their children to receive First Communion? How can parish ministers more effectively assist parents in their faith formation? To what degree is this rite of passage a critical time for parents and their children?
- If you are asked to set up a process whose purpose is to develop greater parish awareness of establishing key rites of passage to ritualize transitions in parishioners' lives, where would you begin? What elements would you include? How could developing this process make a difference in your parish?

This chapter considered growth and change. The joys, celebrations, and accomplishments associated with life transitions and rites of passage coming from growth and change are considered in Chapter Seven.

CHAPTER SEVEN

Joys, Celebrations, and Accomplishments

This chapter considers key life experiences associated with joys, accomplishments, and celebrations, which afford Christians the opportunity to share Jesus' love at key moments.

We begin taking a deeper look by

- → telling the story of my Dad's coming home from the hospital;
- → looking at joy, accomplishment, and celebration;
- → considering Jesus as our model;
- → seeing joys, accomplishments, and celebrations as opportunities for faith formation.

Next, we examine the main points in this chapter. Finally, we offer some discussion questions.

Take a Deeper Look

Joy brings an interruption of human activity and connects with core needs. It springs from the deepest sentiments of the heart and has little to do with monetary achievement, success, or pleasure. We see it manifested in the love of an elderly couple holding hands; the expression of a mother gazing at the face of her newborn child; or the realization that a sick father will be with his family for one more Christmas, reflected in the following episode.

> My father spent ninety days in the hospital, suffering from congestive heart failure. He was resuscitated once, after which he changed. He seemed to be living in another world of deep joy. The family witnessed his ups and downs, not knowing which day would be his last. The doctors and nurses gave up much hope for his recovery.
>
> Then, one day as I walked into the room he smiled and said, "Hi, Bob," with strength in his voice that I hadn't heard for months. Gradually, his health improved and our hearts burst with new hope. The nurses called him the miracle man. Finally, the doctor said he could go home.
>
> As we drove into our yard, the family dog, Tu Tu, caught sight of Dad and barked loudly. Intense happiness filled me. It sprang from the simple, ordinary action of Dad's return home. Few times have I experienced such joy. This was the last time we brought Dad home after a hospital stay.

No one outside of our family knew our joy in having Dad home. Transition times like this provide special opportunities for parish ministers to support a family and the sick person. Parishes need to ask how they can serve better this growing population of sick, elderly people who live at home or in a nursing home.

Joyful times are occasions to celebrate, but they go deeper than this. We celebrate many things—graduations, birthdays, becoming engaged, and receiving a promotion. Some celebrations, like a wedding, have a more ultimate quality than celebrating a pay raise. True joy comes from deeper emotions, which reflect love and gratitude. Once again, the parish community is challenged to reach out to parishioners when they celebrate such joyful times.

Special celebrations held after a Sunday Mass are great ways to maintain a spirit of care in the entire parish. Parish leaders set the tone for such celebrations by encouraging parishioners to become more sensitive to such occurrences, illustrated in the following episode.

> Sophia, a Catholic high school student, won a national debating contest. She was on television and the local media honored her. Her parish, where she was a lector, congratulated her at a special gathering after the last Mass one Sunday. Many of her friends, who rarely went to Mass, attended. They said afterwards how neat it was that the parish cared. One said, "My parish offers little to teenagers. We really feel out of place, so we don't go. I think I'll start attending Sofia's parish when she reads at Mass."

Parishes that recognize such special achievements of its youth set the foundation for greater parish involvement on their part.

Joys, Celebrations, and Accomplishments

Some accomplishments bring joy; others do not. When we reach a goal, a sense of well-being accompanies it. This happens if a team wins an athletic contest or if a person finishes a tedious task. Joy brings emotional intensity associated with deep feelings. This happened when we brought Dad home after his long illness.

The Bible provides further insights into the nature of joy. The Old Testament associates it with communal celebrations including joyful expressions in cultic worship. We read, "Light dawns for the righteous and joy for the upright of heart" (Psalm 96:11). Celebrations praise God's work in creation or occur after winning a battle.

Joy is expressed also in festive celebrations and in offering sacrifice to God (Deuteronomy 12:12). The ark was brought to the city of David with great rejoicing and "David danced before the Lord with all his might..." (2 Samuel 6:12). A close relationship exists between a celebration and the personal feelings attached to it, particularly at festival times. Special parish celebrations at such times can support individual members and inspire the entire community.

Joy in the New Testament, rooted in the Old Testament, is connected with Jesus.

St. Paul links joy with boasting in the saving actions of Christ and his cross. He says, "May I never boast of anything except the cross of our Lord Jesus Christ, by which the world has been crucified to me, and I to the world" (Galatians 6:14). New Testament writers differ from the Hebrew authors in associating joy with suffering and salvation (*Interpreter's Dictionary of the Bible*, v. 2, p. 1000). In this context,

- joy is associated with God's conquest of evil through the power of Jesus' cross;
- joy transforms human weakness and shows the reason for true joy; and
- Jesus is the real motive for our joy. As Paul says, "So I will boast all the more gladly of my weakness, so that the power of Christ may dwell in me" (2 Corinthians 12:9).

The parish community witnesses with great joy the power of the community during the admission of candidates and catechumens into the church at the Easter Vigil. It's as if the joy experienced by early Christians, realizing that Jesus continued to live among them after Pentecost, enters the entire assembly. Christian joy is a gift of the Holy Spirit. Because Jesus died and rose for us, God's Spirit can bring us joy no matter what happens. Christian ministers do well to remember this when difficulties beset them, their families, or the Christian community.

Joy accompanies celebration by the community.

At the beginning of Jesus' life, the angel told the shepherds, "I am bringing good news of great joy for all the people: to you is born this day in the city of David a Savior, who is the Messiah, the Lord" (Luke 2:10–11). In hearing the angel's word, the shepherds sought out the child and celebrated with the Holy Family. All humans celebrate. We celebrate with joy at transition times, like a child's baptism or First Communion. We celebrate joyfully when doing well at work, graduating from school, or winning a prize. We celebrate when knowing that a deceased loved one is now at peace with God.

Connecting joy and suffering with Christ's enables pastoral ministers to recognize what Paul says, "that all of us who have been baptized into Christ Jesus were baptized into his death" (Romans 6:3). When we glory in Christ's cross, it becomes ours. His death and resurrection reveal that death is a way station on the journey to eternity. This realization challenges pastoral ministers to celebrate the joys of others. When celebrating joyfully, the transitory nature of the world's joys are faint reflections of eternal joy with God.

Jesus as Model

How did Mary see Jesus' birth? Imagine her joy as she awaited his coming into the world. We get a glimpse of it in the Magnificat, "My soul proclaims the greatness of God and my spirit rejoices in God my savior" (Luke 1:46–47). How great was her joy when she spoke to Joseph about Jesus during her pregnancy or when she visited Elizabeth. Her pregnancy celebrated what God would accomplish through her son.

Imagine Mary's joy, when Jesus was born and the shepherds and magi visited him. Did she hope that more people would come to celebrate this earth-changing event? Jesus' birth in near isolation from the world reminds us to support needy people who experience joyful or difficult times. Like the shepherds and magi, we can show them love.

When Jesus became an adult, he celebrated with his friends at the marriage feast of Cana. Jewish weddings were joyous events that celebrated a couple's love and the promise of progeny. Jesus, his mother, and other friends were there when the couple ran out of wine. Mary's sensitivity saved the day. This story contains an important lesson for pastoral ministers by encouraging them to act without being asked, when others are in need. Sensitive Christians anticipate what is happening and reach out as Mary did at the wedding feast.

Jesus takes the initiative with the woman at the well seeing her need for conversion. He also anticipates Zacchaeus' desire to change his life and says, "Zacchaeus, hurry and come down, for I must stay at your house today" (Luke 9:5). When people approach Jesus, he recognizes their plight and shows his care. This happens with the woman with the issue of blood and the ten lepers, and Lazarus. Jesus could claim that he is too busy. He does not have to make the journey to see Lazarus, but recognizes, instead, the need and responds accordingly. Because he does, healing occurs, joy comes, and those involved celebrate God's marvels.

Jesus' Paschal Mystery freed us from Adam's sin and won eternal salvation for all. When early Christians realized this, their lives changed, as they rejoiced in the glories of Jesus' cross and the wonders of his resurrection. They realized the implications of Jesus' words in the Sermon on the Mount, "Blessed are you when people revile you and persecute you and utter all kinds of evil against you falsely on my account. Rejoice and be glad, for your reward is great in heaven" (Matthew 5:11–12).

The root of Christian joy is found in Jesus' suffering and death on the cross.

During transition times, pastoral ministers can remember that real joy is rooted in the cross. Without it, we cannot fathom the mystery of suffering. Jesus' suffering and death devastated his disciples, but something special happened at his resurrection. We read, Mary Magdalene and the other Mary "…left the tomb quickly with fear and great joy and ran to tell the disciples" (Matthew 28:8). This joy reached its zenith on Pentecost and persisted in the early church, as Jesus' disciples anticipated his Second Coming. This is reflected in John's words, "…so that you also may have fellowship with us and truly our fellowship is with the Father and with his Son Jesus Christ. We write these things so that our joy may be complete" (1 John 1:3–4).

The first Christians connected joy with faith in Jesus, even though a public profession of faith often brought them severe punishment or martyrdom. They were convinced that happiness rested only in God. Speaking of the Christians at Macedonia, Paul writes, "…during a severe ordeal of affliction, their abundant joy and their extreme poverty have overflowed in a wealth of generosity on their part" (2 Corinthians 8:2). The Scriptures teach us that true joy and celebration are

- connected with Jesus' cross, which paid the price for sin and won our salvation;
- associated with our life with God and are not found in human achievement alone;
- linked with our responsibility to minister to the poor and disenfranchised;

- joined with invitations to help those in need;
- opportunities that offer insights into the mystery of suffering and the dying and rising of Jesus.

Parishes need to celebrate important life events, for such celebrations prepare us for our eternal celebration with God. We look to the virtues that Jesus practiced, especially faith and temperance, for assistance.

Faith

As we see Jesus through Mary's eyes, we picture a man totally committed to his Father's will, even when he did not understand why. This was true also of his mother. How often did she shake her head wondering *why*, as Scribes and Pharisees opposed him and townspeople tried to kill him (Luke 4:29–30)? Did she wonder *why* when Jesus was scourged, carried his cross, and died? Yet, her faith remained firm. Like Jesus, Mary is an example of deep faith. Just as Jesus gave her the grace to remain faithful in suffering, so he blesses us in a similar way.

Reflecting on Jesus' life helps Christians and pastoral ministers deal with rejection, suffering, and death. He shows us the way by forgiving his enemies. When one of Jesus' followers cut off the ear of the high priest's servant with his sword, Jesus told him to put his weapon away (Matthew 26:50–56). Then, Jesus showed the supreme act of forgiveness by dying on the cross.

Temperance

People celebrate at weddings or special yearly events, like New Year or Super Bowl parties. Celebration is natural to life, but true joy comes from celebrating with prudence not from celebrating without bounds. This is manifested at some weddings, when conflicting values can move some couples to celebrate with extravagance. Parish ministers can advise them to keep their wedding in a good balance, focusing on the spiritual aspects of marriage, rather than on the lavishness of the celebration. Where is the virtue of temperance in a celebration that puts a large debt on a family or couple? How do such celebrations relate to Jesus' words, "Blessed are the poor in spirit…blessed are those who hunger for and thirst for righteousness…." (Matthew 5:3, 6)?

Christians today need a strong dose of Christian temperance.

Lavish celebrations may be great fun, take place in exquisite surroundings, and offer rich food and expensive entertainment. Externals, however, do not bring deep joy. Extravagance without solid roots may signal potential problems later in a marriage.

Jesus provides our model of Christian temperance. Seen through Mary's eyes, imagine her joy when her son prepared to celebrate his final Passover. He manifested the temperance of a devout Jew. What was her reaction at the Last Supper when he gave his disciples his body and blood to eat and drink? We need to celebrate with the spirit of Jesus, not the spirit of the world. True celebration has little to do with the money spent or the location. It is influenced by the faith of the people and the love they celebrate. This applies to all life transitions involving rites of passage, like graduations, birthdays, and retirements. Jesus gives us the model to follow.

Faith Formation

Businesses often reward personal accomplishments. Corporations pay bonuses for successful work, and top executives often receive huge payments during profitable financial cycles. Frequently, these bonuses go down the line from corporate officers to managers, secretaries, and custodians. Celebrations often accompany them, usually in the form of parties and time off.

The parish needs celebrations of various sorts. These set the stage for faith celebrations, like the Mass and sacraments. Jesus gave us the example, as he celebrated with his friends. Celebrating transition times, like moving to a new home, beginning a new job, or getting a promotion at work, are occasions for pastoral ministers to enhance faith formation.

To celebrate requires participation of the whole person, not just the mind.

Moving to a New Home

> Daryn did well in business, being promoted to corporate vice president in his mid-thirties. Soon afterward, he, Alicia, his wife, and their daughters moved into a new home, registered in the local Catholic parish, and attended Sunday liturgy there. They were never contacted by the parish and rarely greeted at Mass. In the meantime, colleagues from work asked Daryn and Alicia to attend a flourishing evangelical community several miles away. When they went, the congregation congratulated them on moving into a new home. After that welcome, the family struggled to decide whether to join this community or stay in their Catholic parish.

The parish and pastoral staff could have welcomed Daryn and Alicia and done everything the evangelical community did. The answer for a celebratory parish is not size, but style. Catholic parish ministers need to invite new parishioners to become active parish members. Research studies suggest where to start and how to proceed, but it takes the leadership of a committed pastor and the cooperation of the ministry team to do so. The Gallup organization is linking with parishes and other groups to offer suggestions to enhance parish life. Using the results of their research, parishes may consider anew how to change somewhat engaged parishioners into fully engaged ones (Winseman, Albert and others. *Living Your Strengths*, Catholic Edition, Gallup Press, 2006).

Parish ministers need to be sensitive to transition times, like moving to a new home, as entry points for ministry. When hearing a new parishioner has moved into St. Edmund's parish, the pastor, Fr. Koslewski, takes notice. Sometimes, he meets them at Sunday Mass or parish members inform him when new people have moved into the neighborhood. He also looks at new home listings in the parish from real estate companies.

After he gets a newcomer's name, address, and phone number, he personally visits each new Catholic in his parish. He brings them a gift and asks if he can bless their home. From these visits, he learns about them and their willingness to serve the parish. During these visits, he uncovers many problems, like unemployment, divorce, and marriage outside of the church, or family issues. At vacation time, he hires college students to take a census of the entire neighborhood. Pastoral ministers follow up these visits if people express interest in the Catholic Church or other matters. He makes newcomers feel welcome, visits them, and expresses interest in their families. Because of this outreach, many people join the parish who otherwise would have gone elsewhere.

Parishes need to become more welcoming places, for people continue to leave the church, searching for more welcoming communities. In this regard, pastoral ministers can ask:

- How do we welcome people?
- How do we make them feel at home?
- When do we place too much effort on externals and fail to let the Spirit come through our responses?

Welcome involves more than the priest standing in the back of church each Sunday and welcoming people. Hospitality happens in a communal context. A long-time parishioner once said, "Parishioners stand around after Mass and talk, but who do they talk to? They talk to their friends. As far as they are concerned, I am an outsider and do not exist. I've been in this parish for twenty years, and most parishioners don't know my name."

Moving to a new home is a significant transition time. Some parishes celebrate such times. An announcement welcoming newcomers is a beginning. In addition, a parish minister, volunteer, or neighbor can call on them, visit their home, welcome them, and give details about parish activities. In welcoming parishes, Catholics living on the same street may visit their new neighbors, deliver a packet containing parish information, and welcome them to the church. Some parishes have a welcome event for new members twice yearly.

Beginning a New Job or Getting a Promotion

College graduates often place a priority on finding a high-paying job. They sometimes hope for a starting salary higher than their professors. The desire for money can easily become their monitor for success. For some people, no matter how much money they make, it is not enough to satisfy them. This mentality reflects the value that society places on financial rewards.

Some parish ministers help parishioners address issues like making money and using it wisely. In other places, parishes rarely give parishioners opportunities to sort out their values in a Christian community context.

Job changes are transition times involving new work responsibilities. Many parishioners need help in sorting out such issues. Parish ministers can create a forum to assist parishioners contemplating a job change or seeking new employment. This may include information about whom to contact and how to write a résumé.

> Lay pastoral ministers are encouraged to address questions with parishioners about changing jobs, for these often involve pastoral matters.

Parish volunteers with expertise in job placement or with knowledge of employment opportunities in their companies can assist those looking for new work. One parish matches those seeking employment with job openings that parish members identify in their workplace. Such efforts indicate that the parish cares. Job changes are opportunities for faith formation. Regarding job transitions, the following are recommended for pastoral staffs:

- Establish a ministry for advising parishioners who seek a job change or promotion. Each parish has numerous professional business persons, including psychologists and social workers, who may be available to volunteer their gifts and skills to make this happen.
- Create a welcoming forum to acknowledge parishioners who get promotions or new employment. If they have no objections, recognize them publicly in the bulletin, at Mass, or some other way.
- Offer counseling to help parishioners get advice on a job recently accepted, difficulties on the job, or challenges that a job presents to family life.
- Provide a way that a parishioner looking for a job or seeking a change in occupation can connect with parishioners who know of openings in their companies or elsewhere.

Parish ministers can help parishioners look at job change through the eyes of Christ, not the world. In this process, the Eucharist affords us many insights.

Christian Sacramental Rites of Passage

This section considers the Eucharist as a Christian rite of passage. It is the focal point of Catholic life and worship and helps us appreciate Jesus' presence among us during changing times.

Eucharist

Baptism, confirmation, and Eucharist are sacraments of Christian initiation. The *Rite of Christian Initiation* (RCIA) says, "In the sacraments of Christian initiation we are freed from the power of darkness and joined to Christ's death, burial, and resurrection" (RCIA, #1). Appreciating one's baptism is a lifelong task. We grow into our baptism as we mature in the faith.

It's easy to see baptism as a rite of initiation, for it usually occurs at the beginning or near the start of a person's life. What about the Eucharist? It, too, is a rite of initiation. All Christian activity flows from and leads back to it. The *Catechism of the Catholic Church* says, the Eucharist "is the source and summit of the Christian life" (#1324, quoting *Lumen Gentium*, #11). The Eucharist is the font from which all graces flow and makes new the graces of baptism. When celebrating it, we continually are initiated into the saving mysteries of Jesus' death and resurrection.

Jesus' grace, poured forth daily from the ministries of Word and Eucharist, reminds us of the values that Christians are to live by, as we journey from birth to death. Because of the Eucharist's significance, we celebrate it at core moments involving Christian sacramental rites of passage. These include baptism, confirmation, marriage, orders, penance, and anointing of the sick. Eucharist often is part of the celebration of some non-sacramental rites of passage, like anniversaries, births, deaths, and graduations. The Eucharist is central to every significant Christian rite of passage.

Jesus' suffering and death, which brought about our redemption, is an ongoing reality. At the Last Supper, Jesus commanded his disciples to celebrate the Eucharist in his memory. It celebrates

Jesus' ongoing love, revealed in his suffering, death, and resurrection and helps us connect faith with ordinary and extraordinary life events. Pastoral ministers can help parishioners appreciate how the Eucharist relates to all significant activities, since the birth, death, and resurrection dynamic permeates all creation. They are encouraged, also, to help parishioners better appreciate that they assemble on Sunday to celebrate the Eucharist and to join their dying and rising with that of Jesus. From one day to the next, the Eucharist helps us face life's challenges. As an infinite font of God's grace, it enables us to enter into intimate union with Jesus and inspires us to grow in love, justice, and holiness.

Eucharist is the sacrament par excellence of everyday life.

THE MAIN POINTS IN THIS CHAPTER

- Joyful events provide special opportunities for parish ministers to support the person involved and rejuvenate the parish. In this regard, pastoral ministers can ask how they can better serve the growing population of sick or elderly people who live at home or in nursing homes.
- Joy in the New Testament, built on the teaching of the Old Testament concerning joy, is connected with Jesus. The parish community witnesses the power of Christian communal joy during the initiation of candidates and catechumens into the church at the Easter Vigil.
- Connecting joy and suffering with Christ's enables us to recognize, as Paul says, "that all of us who have been

baptized into Christ Jesus were baptized into his death" (Romans 6:3).

- At all life's moments, especially key transition times, we need loved ones for support and a strong dose of Christian temperance.
- True celebration, which has little to do with money spent or location, is influenced by people's faith and the love they share. As a human institution, the parish needs celebrations of various sorts to touch people's experiences. To celebrate requires participation of the whole person, not just the mind. Pastoral ministers can keep this in the forefront, especially as they prepare liturgical celebrations.
- Celebrating transition times, like moving to a new home, beginning a new job, or getting a promotion at work, are fine occasions for parish faith formation. To have time for such ministries, many Catholic pastoral leaders may have to eliminate organizational clutter.
- Parish ministers can help parishioners address issues like making money and using it wisely. Job changes also are opportunities for parish faith formation.
- Eucharist is the sacrament *par excellence* of everyday life. It is central to every significant Christian rite of passage. In the Eucharist, the church celebrates Jesus' suffering and death as an ongoing reality.
- Pastoral ministers can help parishioners see that they assemble on Sunday, the day when Jesus rose from the dead, to celebrate the Eucharist and join his dying and rising with their dyings and risings.

As a group talk about this chapter using these questions:

- Identify rites of passage that brought you joy and celebration. Why were they important? Who did you want to be there to celebrate with you? How can you connect such these times with your Christian faith and the church?

- Discuss the nature of Christian joy and identify key events that bring you joy. Indicate why these are important for you and others.
- St. Paul says that we must glory in the cross of Jesus. What does this mean, and how can Jesus' cross bring us joy?
- Cite instances in the New Testament that hint at Mary's joy. Discuss the following statement, "The Christian associates joy with salvation, not with feeling good or receiving an earthly reward."
- Why is faith in Jesus necessary for Christian joy? How is temperance connected with joy? How are these virtues associated with rites of passage that flow from human accomplishment?
- Discuss a cultural rite of passage associated with a human accomplishment that provides an opportunity for faith formation. Reflect on rites of passage associated with moving to a new home or beginning a new job as opportunities for faith formation.
- How is the Eucharist a powerful sacrament of the ongoing presence of the Lord in Christian life? How does it sustain us during joyful and difficult transition times? How does it challenge us to be Eucharist for others by regarding all people as brothers and sisters?

Joy and celebration are important. We also experience tragedy as we journey to our final destination. Chapter Eight reflects on tragedy as a part of life.

CHAPTER EIGHT

Tragedies on the Way

This chapter considers life experience associated with human tragedies, including transition times and rites of passage, as people adjust and move on. Such times provide Christians the opportunity to share Jesus' love.

We begin taking a deeper look by

- → telling the story of the tornado;
- → looking at tragedy itself;
- → considering Jesus as our model to imitate;
- → seeing tragedies as opportunities for faith formation.

Next, we examine the main points in this chapter. Finally, we offer some discussion questions.

Take a Deeper Look

The wind's velocity increased as Steve's car snaked its way down the narrow road and approached the river. A steep, wooded hill concealed the beautiful plateau at its top, which overlooked the Ohio River in Indiana. With time to spare on this warm afternoon, Steve stopped by the roadside and walked to the top of the hill. As he did so, the wind intensified, threatening to knock him down. At the summit, he stood for a few moments and witnessed the panorama of the river flowing westward, until it disappeared among the trees several miles away. Before long, limbs broke from black locust trees and leaves and debris slapped Steve in the face. As the rain intensified, he hurried to get to his car, walking past the trees on the downward slope of the hill.

By the time Steve returned to his car, a severe thunderstorm soaked him. As he drove away, strewn tree limbs covered the road. When he arrived at the next small town he stopped at a restaurant to dry off. After he entered the restroom a man covered with blood opened the door. Steve asked if he was okay. The man said, "Yes, my cuts are from glass fragments from the tornado." Then Steve realized what had happened. He missed the brunt of a tornado and drove through its aftermath. Steve said, "Where did the tornado hit?" The man replied, "Right along the road you drove. How come you didn't get caught in it?" At that moment, Steve sensed that if he had not stopped to walk to the hilltop, he would have been near the eye of the tornado instead of on its periphery. It came down the road at the precise time he was on the hill.

> Returning home, Steve turned on the radio and learned that this tornado devastated the whole area. Story after story appeared in the newspaper the next day, describing tragedies resulting from this tornado. A boyhood friend died, while making deliveries for a food chain. A family had the basement door of their home blown off. Upon entering the basement, they found a terrified horse, alive and healthy, cowering in the corner.

The tornado story introduces this chapter on life's tragedies. Many tragedies are just as unanticipated as the tornado. When they come, they affect us personally, spiritually, and professionally. At such times, a parish's support is essential. Just as thousands of volunteers assisted these tornado victims, so must parish ministers and parishioners support their vulnerable brothers and sisters when tragedies occur.

Life Moments: Tragedy

The word *tragedy* has its roots in a Greek word *tragoidia*, possibly referring to a *goat-song* or the *song of a goat*. Its origins are unsure. Some believe that it originated from actors in a Greek tragedy robed in goatskins. Others say it goes back to sacrificing a goat in fertility rituals associated with the god Dionysus. Still others say it relates to seasonal rituals, often connected with suffering and death.

From etymological history two things are significant.

1. Like the ancient wisdom says, tragedies make no more sense than a goat singing. Those with knowledge of goats find it hard to imagine them singing. Such a notion seems nonsensical. Little wonder, then, that this word was associated with experiences like a tornado, a hurricane, or the sudden death of a young, vibrant person. These events, too,

make no more sense than a goat singing. The term gives us insight into how sad such experiences are for those struck by them.

2. Tragedies often are associated with sacrifice. In the Old Testament, after putting the sins of the people on a goat, it was sent into the desert (Leviticus 16:8–10, 20–22). Christians see this action as foreshadowing Jesus' taking upon himself the sins of the world and offering his life as a sacrifice for them. This, too, makes no sense to human reason. Who could imagine that the all-powerful creator of heaven and earth humbled himself to the point of death for our sins? Jesus' sacrifice, the greatest tragedy in all history, makes our tragedies more tolerable.

Tragedies occur throughout creation. They affect the plant, animal, and human worlds. The world was weakened, not corrupted, by Original Sin. From a Christian perspective, tragedies occur, not because of a punishing God but because of human sin and earthly imperfections. In a broken world, they interrupt the ever-flowing love of an all-good God. This same God stands beside us to strengthen us during tragic occurrences. Nature is full of tragic events. One occurred recently at Sam's Indiana farm.

> For nearly forty years, he enjoyed the beautifully proportioned tulip poplar tree that stood majestically on the top of the third ridge, near the back of the land. Thirty-five years before, a conservation official had bored into this tree to ascertain its age.
>
> From his data, Sam concluded that the tree was one hundred years old. It was about 150 feet tall and fifty inches across at eye height. Since it fought its way through the other trees to reach for the light, no branch protruded from its sides for nearly one hundred feet from the ground. As it ascended above the

> other trees, its leafy canopy invited those walking nearby to examine its stately nature.
>
> In July, as Sam walked the woods, he knew something had happened. When he looked for the tree's canopy, it was not there. He first thought a tree poacher cut the tree. Then, as he gazed into the maze of trees surrounding it, he saw its ripped and shredded top, lying beside its base. The once proud tree was now a dead trunk, broken apart and cut into pieces, still standing on the forest floor. Pieces of tree bark were flung for hundreds of feet in every direction like confetti. The tree's top was upside down, leaning against its trunk. The trunk split into four or five parts near the bottom. In a flash, one powerful lightning bolt had destroyed this beautiful, stately tree. As it stands now, it is too dangerous to remove and too broken to use for anything except forest fertilizer. Gradually the tree will rot and return to the earth from which it came.

This tragic event is repeated millions of times in the earth's forests and fields. Nature includes many such tragedies. Is it any wonder, then, that humans are victims of tragedies? Our tragedies are different. They happen because of sin and nature's imperfection. In such a world, clashes occur, sometimes bringing sad, painful consequences. For example:

- Imperfections of birth leave children scarcely able to survive because of deformities.
- Circumstances, like a drunken parent or violent friend, lead to serious physical and mental issues.
- Teenagers, after partying, lose their lives in a car accident.
- An all-star high school student, drugged at a party and injected with cocaine, ends up as a hopeless addict.

- Military personnel serving our country receive injuries resulting in temporary and sometimes permanent paralysis.
- A woman has a miscarriage.
- One spouse abandons the other one for a younger partner.

Human tragedies cross all boundaries. Tragedies exist everywhere, and pastoral ministers can recognize them as significant transition times and ritualize them with rites of passage. They open up possibilities for new life directions, as exemplified in Jan and Colin's story.

> This young married couple looked forward to their child's birth. In time, Jan and Colin learned they would have twins. At birth, each child was sickly and weighed less than two pounds. Neither was given much chance to live, but their parents maintained an endless vigil with the children. Once, a visitor remarked, "Isn't it tragic that they are not healthy children. Jan and Colin are such good parents."
>
> The parents received support from their parish and pastoral minister who visited, consoled, and prayed with them. Their lives changed to take care of the children, Alyson and Kirt. Week by week, the babies grew stronger and four months later they left the hospital for home.

The power of prayer, the miracle of modern science, and the dedication of Jan and Colin kept the children alive. This initial tragic event of two sickly children, who a few years earlier would not have lived, was a transition time that forever changed their parents' lives. Today, Alyson and Kirt are happy, healthy children. The family is very grateful to the pastoral minister and parish who supported them.

For Christians, human tragedies can be seen in light of the tragedy of Jesus' sacrificial death. No matter how much we suffer, it cannot compare with the suffering of the Son of God. Jesus loves us and invites us to join our sufferings to his. Pastoral ministers assist hurting people greatly when they focus on Jesus Christ during tragic times.

Just as Jesus needed his mother's love at the foot of the cross, so we need support in our tragedies. Tragic life transitions afford key moments for pastoral ministers to extend a loving outreach to the needy as they remember the words of Paul to Timothy,

> If we have died with him, we will also live with him;
> if we endure, we will also reign with him;
> if we deny him, he will also deny us;
> if we are faithless, he also remains faithful—
> for he cannot deny himself. (2 Timothy 2:11–13)

Jesus as Model

Human poverty is a great tragedy. Since it is so prevalent all over the globe, we tend to pass it by. Our tendency is to respond more directly to dramatic tragic occurrences, like Hurricane Katrina or the attack on the Twin Towers. It's easy to miss ordinary life tragedies, like violence, manipulation, and famine, or to become hardened to them, as we often do to poverty in city slums.

Jesus did not justify, excuse, or downplay poverty. He condemned it as he reached out to impoverished people, regardless of whether their poverty was economic (blind beggar), physical (leper), psychological (disturbed man), or spiritual (woman at the well). In so doing, he showed solicitude for those caught in poverty's cycle.

In third world countries, people sustain themselves and help others with the few resources they have, as reflected in this story.

Loving parish ministers, professional and volunteer, are powerful symbols of the compassionate Christ.

Sonta, a middle aged woman, lives with her two children in a small impoverished village near Mexico City. A small plot of land surrounds their two-room house, and a shed and chicken coop are attached to it. One afternoon, Kathy, a college student from America serving as a volunteer pastoral minister, visited them. She and Sonta sat on the front porch with her two children. As they enjoyed one another's company, a stranger approached them. Sonta welcomed the woman and invited her to join them. The visitor asked her for a few eggs to feed her own family. Disappointed that she had none to share with the woman, Sonta stood up and walked around the back of her house. When returning, she carried a full-grown chicken in a box, which she gave to the visitor.

As the stranger left, Sonta told her children, "We'll sacrifice for a while, for we used to eat eggs from this chicken. Don't worry, though. God will take care of us. Jesus taught us to share what we have with others in need. The needy woman who visited us today represented Jesus, who comes to us in every hungry person. When we are generous to the needy, we are good to Jesus; when we reject them, we reject him." (story from Gina Meyer, used with permission)

Pastoral ministers can learn much from such stories, for tragedies happen every day. Hence, if pastoral ministers appreciate tragedy in ordinary circumstances, they can better see it in the larger scope of life and better appreciate Christ's role in redeeming the human race from the cycle of tragedy.

In human tragedies, pastoral ministers do well to reflect on the Scriptures, especially Jesus' life. They can begin by meditating on how Jesus felt in difficult circumstances and how he responded. They may consider, also, how a present tragedy looks in light of how Jesus dealt with tragedies, as seen through the eyes of his mother. When he cured the sick and raised up the dead, did her heart burst with joy? Deep down, did she realize that his Father sent him to overcome people's tragic condition through his life and death?

What happened when things turned against Jesus? Imagine Mary's reaction, as she witnessed Jesus' arrest, scourging, and crowning with thorns. To the bystander and his disciples, such events were tragic. But what were they like for Mary? Did she remember the words of Simeon, who said,

> This child is destined for the falling and rising of many in Israel, and to be a sign that will be opposed so that the inner thoughts of many will be revealed—and a sword will pierce your own soul too. (Luke 2:35)

By conquering tragedy through love, Jesus is the model of a tragic hero who laughs in the face of human brokenness. So can pastoral ministers, when dealing with tragic situations in ministry. Figuratively, Mary may have heard the *goat singing* when Jesus' death brought humankind new life. It's one thing for a disciple to witness the suffering and death of a master. It's another, if this disciple is his mother with knowledge that her son is the Son of God.

Is there a greater paradox in human history than the Son of God dying for us? With good reason, the church celebrates Mary as the one who best understands the tragedy of Jesus' redemption. Jesus' death, viewed through her eyes, helps explain why ordinary Christians, who patiently endure tragedy, often invoke Mary for support. Did she not know that Jesus took upon himself the world's brokenness? She is the compassionate Mother of God reaching out to a broken world. It is not surprising that Mary appears to simple people, like Bernadette at Lourdes or Juan Diego at Guadalupe.

More than other human beings, Mary knows the depths of tragedy, for she witnessed it in her son.

Looking at tragedy in relation to Jesus' death, we know that Jesus loves us, Mary is our intercessor, and we are to address human tragedies with faith. We reflect further on tragic events in Jesus' life by considering the virtues of justice, fortitude, and prudence.

Justice

Jesus made right the wrong of Adam's sin that brought injustice into the world. The first message he taught when beginning his public ministry was one of justice. He says,

> The Spirit of the Lord is upon me
> because he has anointed me
> to bring good news to the poor.
> He has sent me to proclaim release to the captives
> And recovery of sight to the blind,
> To let the oppressed go free,
> To proclaim the year of the Lord's favor. (Luke 4:18–19)

When speaking of the end of the world, Jesus says,

> Come you that are blessed of my Father, inherit the kingdom prepared for you from the foundation of the world; for I was hungry and you gave me food, I was thirsty and you gave me something to drink. I

> was a stranger and you welcomed me....Truly I tell you, just as you did it to one of the least of these who are members of my family, you did it to me. (Matthew 25:34–40)

Justice is not an option for Christians but their deepest responsibility. As *Justice in the World* says, "Action on behalf of justice and participation in the transformation of the world fully appear to us as a constitutive dimension of the preaching of the Gospel..." (Introduction).

Pastoral ministers grow in insight when they realize that without a justice component, preaching God's Word and ministry are incomplete. Jesus' death on the cross is the foundation for Christian justice. He is the reason we must be just. As members of his body, we must treat every person as he does. The church is not really Christian if it is not committed to justice.

Fortitude

Imagine Mary's reaction as many disciples left, after Jesus promised to give them the bread of life (John 6:66–68). Shortly before this, Jesus fed thousands of hungry people with bread and fish. When he told them that they do not live by bread alone, they rejected him. Was Mary reassured at Jesus' fortitude, as he refused to back down? Consider also her feelings as rumors surfaced that Jewish leaders sought his death. Did she discuss the matter with Jesus? Through growing tensions, Mary showed remarkable courage. Reflect on her fortitude as Jesus was taken in the Garden of Gethsemane and dragged before Roman leaders in preparation for his death (Matthew 26:36–57).

Imagine, too, her courage when Jesus passed by her carrying his cross and when she heard the cruel sounds of the soldiers nailing him to a tree. Such events took Mary to the limits of human endurance. She knew the depths of such tragic actions. When Jesus took his last breath, it took courage for Mary to walk away with hope, convinced that her son accomplished his mission, for the whole drama said otherwise. What lessons can pastoral ministers learn from Mary's fortitude, when life appears bleak and they wonder why they should go on?

> Prudence means acting with moderation, based on the wisdom to regulate one's actions through reason and good judgment.

The early disciples manifested similar courage, as they boldly proclaimed Jesus' message after Pentecost. Often, this led to imprisonment and death. Subsequent generations of Christians showed remarkable fortitude in facing martyrdom and suffering. The example of Jesus, Mary, and the saints offers us courage. In them, we see that God's love conquers all, if we believe and maintain hope.

Prudence

Tragic events require prudence, as revealed through the lives of Jesus and Mary. They knew when to speak and when to be silent. Mary was not a hysterical disciple, bewailing Jesus' arrest, conviction, and death. She teaches us that in tragedy, silence is often the best response. During Jesus' final agony, he said little. He knew his inevitable fate and taught us how a mature person responds. Maturity means knowing what situations demand our response and which do not. As a wise woman once said, "I pick my battles. When my actions do nothing except frustrate me, I remain silent."

During Jesus' last days, he showed prudence to an eminent degree. He rejected a disciple's recourse to physical violence, when this disciple cut off a soldier's ear. After a Roman court accused him, he said little. Like Jesus, the wise person keeps prudence in the forefront and refrains from actions that will be regretted afterward.

Faith Formation

Pastoral ministers can get so busy that they take little time to consider deep values and issues. Busyness engulfs parents, pastoral ministers, and children. This pattern begins in childhood. One high school student said, "We are caught up in what we do and have little time to think deeply about what we believe. Our assignments in religion class touch our lives. As we discuss them, we do something that we rarely do outside of class. We consider our values and faith."

Tragedies sometime interrupt our busy lives. When they strike, life comes to a halt. This occurs at the death of a loved one, a sudden sickness, or a hurricane's devastation. The more devastating the tragedies are, the greater the opportunity to help those affected. Pastoral ministers need to be sensitive during tragic times, which include:

- sickness or death of a spouse, child, or parent;
- a serious automobile or other accident;
- the loss of a job necessary to maintain the family;
- the inability of parents to solve difficulties leading to separation and divorce;
- the discovery of a spouse's infidelity;
- the realization that a teenage child is hooked on drugs;
- an unmarried teenage girl being pregnant;
- a woman considering an abortion.

Such instances afford opportunities for pastoral ministers to help others. They can develop a mentality that zeroes in on such occasions as opportunities to make a difference. Without such an attitude, it's easy to miss the chance to help people move from brokenness to healing. Pastoral ministers are privileged to be able to support grieving people by visiting the sick, bringing communion, offering spiritual consolation, spending time with loved ones after death, going to the funeral parlor, attending the church service, and sending a card.

Pastoral bereavement committees often manifest compassion and expertise, but how much further do their expressions of grief go? Do pastoral ministers follow up a week or a month afterwards? Grieving people need support later on. Does the concern of pastoral ministers during tragic times extend into the future? They are challenged to carry on the initial work they do with sick people by developing a follow-up ministry. In so doing, they support grieving loved ones, as they are healed.

Long-term pastoral ministry to grieving people takes various forms. These extend from an annual remembrance of the dead on All Souls Day to phone calls, visits, cards, or memorial Masses for those who died during the past year. When done effectively, this bears much fruit. People grieve differently. Some move on quickly after a loved one's death. Others do not. It is wise to keep this in mind when helping a grieving person. During hurtful times, the sacraments help us to become whole again and facilitate a return to wholeness.

Christian Sacramental Rites of Passage

Reconciliation

The *Catechism of the Catholic Church* says,

> The Lord Jesus Christ, physician of our souls and bodies, who forgave the sins of the paralytic and restored him to bodily health, has willed that his

> Church continue, in the power of the Holy Spirit, his work of healing and salvation, even among her own members. (#1421)

In the sacrament of reconciliation, we confess our sins to a priest and accept responsibility for the results that they bring. We acknowledge ourselves as sinners, responsible for our sinful actions. When we meditate on Jesus' suffering and accept our role in it, we see the pain we caused him and how our sins bring suffering to others. The sacrament of reconciliation is a powerful rite of passage, moving us from the death caused by sin to the newness of life, made possible through God's grace. This sacrament

- renews us every time we admit our sinfulness, express our sorrow, resolve to do better, and try to make right the wrong we have done;
- helps to heal the broken body of Christ;
- takes us out of ourselves and sends us into the world;
- helps us change our sinful ways, accept our call to discipleship, and fulfill our responsibility to serve our brothers and sisters.

A prayer of the *Rite of Penance* indicates the healing power of this sacrament. It says,

> Lord Jesus Christ,
> you are the Lamb of God;
> you take away the sins of the world.
> Through the grace of the Holy Spirit
> restore me to friendship with your Father.
> cleanse me from every stain of sin
> in the blood you shed for me,
> and raise me to new life
> for the glory of your name. (#91)

THE MAIN POINTS IN THIS CHAPTER

- The word *tragedy* has its roots in a Greek word *tragoidia* probably referring to a *goat-song* or the *song of a goat*. Since tragedies make no more sense than a goat singing, little wonder that this word was associated with experiences, like a tornado, a hurricane, or the sudden death of a young vibrant person. The term gives us insight into how sad such experiences are for those who suffer them.
- Tragedies are associated with sacrifice, reflected in the Old Testament account where after putting the sins of the people on a goat, it was sent into the desert (Leviticus 16:8–10, 20–22). Christians see this latter action as foreshadowing Jesus' taking upon himself the sins of the world and offering his life as a sacrifice for them.
- Pastoral ministers assist hurting people when they focus the Lord Jesus Christ during tragic times. They need to show the same compassion and love as Jesus did.
- Tragedies occur all through nature, and human tragedies happen in many different ways. Jesus shows us that when life seems absurd, more is involved than we can understand. More than other human beings, Mary knows the depths of tragedy, for she witnessed it in her son. She was the courageous one among Jesus' followers. Pastoral ministers grow in wisdom when they better appreciate the tragedies they deal with through the eyes of Jesus and Mary.
- Jesus made right the wrong of Adam's sin, which brought injustice into the world. He reestablished justice, which is the first message that he taught when beginning his public ministry. Justice is not an option for Christians but their deepest responsibility.

- Prudence means acting with moderation, based on the wisdom to regulate one's actions through reason and good judgment. Prudence was manifested during Jesus' last days, when he manifested it to an eminent degree.
- Parish ministers can develop a mentality that zeroes in on tragic occasions. Without such an attitude, it's easy to miss the chance to help people move from brokenness to healing. Pastoral ministers are challenged to avoid the attitude that tragedies are unavoidable, but quickly can be overcome.
- Long term pastoral ministry to grieving people takes various forms—an annual remembrance of the dead on All Souls Day, phone calls, visits, cards, or memorial Masses for those who died during the past year. People grieve differently: some move on quickly after a loved one's death, while others do not.
- Many church sacraments celebrate life's transitions, but one in particular considers sin, the root cause of tragedy. This is the sacrament of reconciliation, penance, or confession.
- The sacrament of reconciliation is a powerful rite of passage, moving us from the death caused by sin to the newness of life, made possible through God's grace.

As a group talk about this chapter using these questions:

- Reflect on *natural* tragedies that affected your life. Why were these significant and what lessons came from them? Who supported you?
- Identify several *personal* tragedies, involving yourself or people close to you that affected your life. What support did you receive from pastoral ministers and the parish community? What did you learn?
- When you hear the description of a tragedy as the "song of

a goat," how do you react? What connections do you see between this expression, the inexplicable nature of human tragedy, and the ministry of a pastoral minister?

- How is the tragedy of Jesus' suffering and death connected with all human tragedy? How can a pastoral minister bring Christ's consolation, hope, and strength to those who suffer?
- Discuss: "Tragedies can bring new directions to a person's life." Cite examples from your life or from those around you.
- Discuss: "All human tragedy must be seen in light of Jesus' sacrificial death."
- Reflect on human poverty as a great world tragedy. How does it symbolize the failure of humans to live by Jesus' commandment to love one another? Cite ways that your ministry helped others deal with their poverty.
- Discuss Jesus' tragedy on the cross and human tragedies through the eyes of Jesus' mother.
- Reflect on sin as the greatest human tragedy. Why is this so, and what are its implications for your ministry?
- Why are justice, fortitude, and prudence necessary during tragic times?
- Discuss the opportunities tragic events provide to pastoral ministers for faith formation.
- Discuss: "Tragedy often has no answers, except I am sorry." Reflect on the connection between personal sin, tragedy, sorrow, and the sacrament of reconciliation. Apply your conclusions to your life and ministry.

The Rite of Penance invites us to turn away from sin and begin anew. Endings and new beginnings occur all through life. They are discussed in Chapter Nine.

CHAPTER NINE

Endings and New Beginnings

This chapter considers key life experiences associated with endings and new beginnings, including transition times and rites of passage, as people adjust and move on. Such times provide opportunities for Christians to share Jesus' love at key moments.

We begin taking a deeper look by

- → telling the story of Jim's Garden;
- → looking at endings and new beginnings;
- → considering Jesus as our model;
- → seeing endings and beginnings as opportunities for faith formation.

Next, we examine the main points in this chapter. Finally, we offer some discussion questions.

Take a Deeper Look

Thirty-five years ago, Jim planted a garden on a small tract of land on Red Hog Pike in Indiana. In the ensuing years, the garden became an important part of his life. He planted it each spring. As the crops grew, he and Joan, his wife, worked side by side. Their young children assisted them. The lessons that the family learned working in the garden became part of them.

Pesky weeds were a constant challenge. Occasionally, when they seemed to overwhelm his garden, Jim's family wondered if he would get any crops. Regardless, he kept up his confidence, hope, and persistence. When Jim's crops matured, he put them in bushel baskets. He proudly showed his family the squash, cabbage, radishes, carrots, tomatoes, lettuce, onions, potatoes, and green beans. He always looked for ways to improve his garden.

Large numbers of deer, turkeys, and raccoons eventually came into the area. Jim loved all nature, especially the animals. Even though they ate his crops, he remained positive. He was disappointed when he watched his garden grow and look beautiful one week but found it seriously chewed up by the animals the next. Yet, Jim never wavered, as he devised new ways to keep them out of the garden. Eventually, he built a high fence around the entire plot. Somehow, the animals got through, but Jim kept trying. His garden was part of who he was and reflected his values. He worked it, no matter how hot or damp it was. He continued with it even as he aged and it became harder for him to breathe and walk.

One afternoon, after weeding his garden on a hot day, when the temperature was well into the nineties, Jim told his wife, "This is my last garden. I can't do it anymore." The same year, late summer faded into fall, and Thanksgiving came.

Jim spent the days following this holiday at the farm with his family. On Saturday afternoon, he visited his friend and neighbor, who sometimes helped him. After they spoke for nearly an hour, Jim said, "This is my last garden." His friend replied, "You've said that before. You'll be back out there next spring." Jim replied, "No, this is my last garden. I wish you would take down all the four-by-four poles that hold up the fencing around the garden and keep them. Then, remove the electric fencing and the battery. I want you to have them. Throw away what's left and bush hog the plot, so that it looks clean and fresh. You have been a good friend and neighbor these thirty years."

As they stood there, his friend sensed a feeling of inevitability and thought, "Jim is folding up his tent in the way he loves." The place where they stood seemed like holy ground. He would soon discover the full flowering of what happened there. Next week, he cleared Jim's garden. It was nicely cut and the ground sparkled in the cool winter air. When Jim learned it was taken care of, he smiled and said, "I'm glad."

Four weeks later on Christmas Eve, after the Christmas dinner and just before they exchanged presents, Jim rose from the table, took a step toward his wife, Joan, and fell to the ground. He died right there. When Jim was laid out, a beautiful basket of yellow roses sat next to the casket, a gift from his friend.

Jim's garden taught his family valuable lessons while they worked side by side. As the children matured, they understood the garden's significance. Jim's family plans to pick out a tree and plant it at the edge of Jim's garden, as a testimony to what he taught them. As this tree grows, they hope to gather around it and recount the stories of the man who loved his garden but loved God and his family more. This tree reminds us of the ancient African custom, described in Chapter One, where grandfathers take their grandsons into the forest to select a tree. Recalling it, we end as we began—with the endless cycle of births and deaths.

The story of Jim's garden reminds pastoral ministers that life is an endless cycle of endings and new beginnings. For people of faith, Jim's death marks the end of life on earth and promises the beginning of a new life with God for all eternity. Jim's eternal destiny after death was his deepest motivating force as he grew up, raised his family, grew old, and died. (story used with permission of Jim's family)

The yearly endings and new beginnings of his garden crops remind us of core truths of faith. Pastoral ministers can learn lessons from the story of Jim and his garden, which include:

- the significance of creation as a fertile ground to experience God's love and life's joys and sorrows;
- the value of using the gifts God gives every person to praise and worship the God who made us;
- the importance of a simple way of life, no matter how complicated the world becomes;
- the opportunities presented by tragic times, like Jim's sudden death, to minister to the families of the deceased.

Effective pastoral ministers recognize such lessons and respond accordingly. Clear perspectives on life's values enable them to see what is really important with wisdom and clarity of thought.

Endings and New Beginnings

When the first red bud trees show their colors in the treetops along the highways, we know spring is near. The ending of the old year, with its winter symbols of death, is replaced with new beginnings. Soon, trees and flowers burst into life as the air warms and the days lengthen.

Remember the first time you saw a newborn baby? As we discussed earlier, a baby is a special member of a family, but a child's specialness goes beyond whose child it is. When reflecting on a newborn child, we ask,

- What human life is not precious?
- What is this specialness that goes beyond the fact that it is your child?
- What makes every child special?
- What is it about small children that reflects a profound mystery and gives us a glimpse into God's eternal designs?

Every child points to life's sacredness. This recognition offers pastoral ministers a foundation from which to reach out to any person celebrating new beginnings or struggling with endings, like death. People of various times and places regarded death and what follows as sacred and developed rituals surrounding it. Until modern times, such rituals pointed to life's sacredness.

How we value death influences our response to lesser endings and beginnings, like going to college, marrying, having a miscarriage, starting a job, being fired, getting sick, and growing old. Secular society looks at such events through materialistic glasses and gives them a secular twist. This leaves our hearts hollow, for secular values cannot provide the golden link that connects life's temporary endings and new beginnings to our final death and the afterlife. Spiritual values provide this link. They bridge the gap between earth and heaven and provide a fundamental life orientation, linking the pieces of a complex life into a whole picture. The human ability to do this reminds us of Gordon W. Allport's words that a *religious philosophy of life* is the most inclusive way to link life's various dimensions into a unified whole (Gordon W. Allport, *The Individual and His Religion*). Only a life philosophy that includes God in the mystery of death can link life's ambiguities into a meaningful pattern.

> Endings, followed by new beginnings, always bring renewed life.

Although the Western world is steeped in functionalism and impersonalism abounds, we meet compassionate people in business offices, schools, warehouses, hospitals, or retirement homes. They offer many opportunities to bring spiritual values into the marketplace, illustrated in the following story.

> When Tanya's husband suffered a serious illness, her boss came to the hospital's intensive care unit. As a manager herself, Tanya wondered about the time that she would have to spend caring for her husband. Her boss said, "Tanya, your main work is with your husband and family. Forget about your job for a while. We will cover for you. Do not work from home or receive e-mail messages from clients." His words greatly consoled her. They also invite pastoral ministers to recommit themselves to showing profound compassion to hurting people. When Tanya returned to work months later, she worked doubly hard for the company that treated her family so well during this critical time.

A great hunger exists to serve others. This permeates all levels of society. We see it in the generosity of college graduates who volunteer a year or two to help in needy areas. Their commitment to serve others helps them fulfill a need for more than money or materialistic possessions.

> Death challenges us to question materialistic norms that distort core values associated with death and the afterlife.

Even when society gives witnesses to compassion, it cannot probe deeply into the motivation for such actions. Here, the Christian message bridges the gap. As Jesus says, "The harvest is plentiful, but the laborers are few; therefore, ask the Lord of the harvest to send out laborers into his harvest" (Matthew 9:37–38).

Our unifying philosophy of life is faith in Jesus Christ. Believing in him enables us to connect our dyings and risings with his death and resurrection. In so doing, we have a reason to live and a reason to die.

Jesus as Model

After Jesus was raised from the dead, his disciples realized that something new had happened. His resurrection promised new life. Initially, the disciples did not know what being raised from the dead meant (Luke 24:6–11). After Jesus ascended to heaven, they waited in anxious concern. When the Holy Spirit descended upon them at Pentecost, they knew that Jesus was alive, not dead. Their rallying cry became "He lives!"—and they understood how. They interpreted Jesus' words about them being part of his body in light of the Pentecost experience. Since they are part of Jesus' body, *he lives through them*. The early Christians saw that

- Jesus is the head, they are the members;

- his risen Spirit pulsates through their flesh and blood experiences;
- he remains in the words and the rituals he left us, especially the Eucharist; and
- he lives through Christians, for his unique risen presence continues until the end of time in his body, the church.

> Without spiritual values that integrate dyings and new beginnings into a consistent pattern, how can the painful and seemingly unfair events that sooner or later beset us make sense?

In the days after Pentecost, Mary's heart burst with joy, as she witnessed the fulfillment of Jesus' mission. Through his birth, life, suffering, death, and resurrection, he won eternal salvation for all who live a good life. Pastoral ministers do well to consider what the endings and new beginnings looked like during Jesus' life, as Mary reflected on them in light of his resurrection. Did she see the ambiguity surrounding Jesus' conception and birth in a new way, as she perceived the whole picture? Imagine her thoughts as she once more reflected on Jesus' birth, circumcision, and early life. Imagine too her feelings, as she again recalled the moment when he left home to accomplish his mission of redemption! Picture Mary talking to Jesus, as he worked miracles, preached, chose his disciples, and aroused the anger of the Roman and Jewish leaders. Never sure of what would happen to him, did not Mary reassure him of her support and God's love? Reflect on what Mary experienced when she looked back on Jesus' final hours, as he began the road to Calvary. Finally, consider the times when we began a new life venture, not certain of the outcome.

As pastoral ministers renew their hope, it is well for then to reflect on two virtues closely associated with Jesus, namely love and gratitude.

Love

No word better captures the feelings surrounding a child's birth than *love*. Mothers risk their life in childbirth so their children can live. Even though childbirth involves pain, the love that comes from bringing a child into the world surpasses the difficulties involved. Parents sacrifice a former lifestyle when a child is born. By becoming parents, they gave up life patterns of a childless couple to assume new parental responsibilities. It is an ending, as well as a beginning. The child's life begins as the parent's previous way of life ends. In reflecting on parenthood, Paul's words to the Corinthians come to mind.

> Love is patient; love is kind; love is not envious or boastful or arrogant or rude. It does not insist on its own way; it is not irritable or resentful; it does not rejoice in wrongdoing, but rejoices in the truth. It bears all things, believes all things, hopes all things, endures all things. (1 Corinthians 13:4–7)

Such love continues throughout life's various endings and new beginnings. On an occasion like graduation, for example, parents show their love by snapping pictures to capture the event. Something similar occurs at weddings, anniversaries, and other life moments. While such endings are joyful, others involve pain, like job loss or sudden death. Then, pastoral ministers can remind grieving people that God's love never wavers, but offers many blessings to those who believe. We grieve the loss of loved ones because we loved them so much.

The story of the prodigal son tells of a father's love. After the younger son demanded his share of the inheritance and squandered it on high living, he returned home penniless.

His father showed his love, which never wavered in spite of what his son did (Luke 15:11–32). The parable reminds us of God's love and helps pastoral ministers see that the Father's love is always there for God's sons and daughters.

Gratitude

Gratitude implies giving thanks. Christians call Jesus' celebration that gives us his body and blood, the *Eucharist*. In Greek, this word means *thanksgiving*, for it expresses our gratitude to the Lord who made and redeems us. Paul says in Ephesians that gratitude moves us to "giving thanks to God the Father at all times and for everything in the name of our Lord Jesus Christ" (5:20).

We often express gratitude more after people die than when they were alive. Grieving survivors often wish they had expressed their thanks while a loved one was living. Some people find gratitude hard to express. Others rarely express gratitude for anything. Why? Perhaps, they never experienced deep love. Since transition times and the rites of passage enable people to start over, pastoral ministers need to be sensitive to them. Beginning anew does not happen overnight as Katie's story illustrates.

> No one knew why Katie couldn't express gratitude and give thanks regardless of what others did for her. When she suffered a serious injury that required hospitalization, Michaela, a coworker, visited her regularly. In time, Katie recovered and resumed her former job.
>
> Michaela's kindness helped Katie be happier and more grateful. Even when Michaela's initial help seemed unappreciated, she persisted. Gradually, Katie realized that Michaela cared for her as a friend, not out of obligation. She learned that friends remain constant in good and difficult times. Gradually, things

changed. Katie eventually shared the reasons why she was aloof. This would not have happened if Michaela hadn't responded lovingly during this critical transition time.

From a faith perspective, each ending and new beginning is an expression of love and reminds us of God's great love.

Faith Formation

The liturgical year with its recurrent cycle of endings and new beginnings reminds us that we can show concern for others on many occasions. The church year ends as Ordinary Time closes in November. Following the feast of Christ the King, the new liturgical cycle begins with Advent, a season of anticipation. On Christmas and Epiphany we celebrate new beginnings with Christ's birth. Then, we move forward, beginning with Lent and moving toward Holy Week. This culminates with Good Friday, when Jesus' life ends and our salvation is won. We begin anew with Jesus' resurrection on Easter and the church's birth on Pentecost.

Throughout the liturgical year, other endings and beginnings remind us of the same life dynamic. These include: lives of the saints, celebrating the end of their earthly life and the beginning of eternal life in heaven; anniversary Masses for the deceased; and special feasts, like the Annunciation, Assumption, Birth of Mary, Triumph of the Holy Cross, Presentation, and the Baptism of Jesus. Endings and new beginnings occur in a variety of ways and include starting school, getting engaged, starting anew after divorce, miscarriage, or a spouse's death.

Endings and new beginnings allow us to show that we care. When my Mom was dying, a woman volunteer sat with her at night to give us relief. Her presence with Mom was her lived vocation. After Mom died, our family was vulnerable and needed support. Pastoral ministers, sensing this, reached out and helped.

Compassionate pastoral ministers make a difference. They help grieving family members be healed, return to the church, or be reconciled. They bring a deeper realization of God's love. When responding with love, pastoral actions reinforce the faith of Catholics and motivate others to a deeper spiritual awareness.

Christian Sacramental Rites of Passage

Endings and new beginnings provide opportunities for parish ministers to counter the superficial messages people receive daily. This can happen at baptism, marriage, as children begin school, or when a person is seriously sick. Spiritual breakthroughs can occur on such occasions, when the veneer of surface living gives way to recognizing that life means more than making money, acquiring possessions, or having a good time.

Sacraments assist people in their quest for a meaningful existence. To this end, pastoral ministers do well to look at endings and new beginnings in light of the sacrament of the anointing of the sick.

Anointing of the Sick

The rite of the anointing of the sick, a sacrament of healing, forgiveness, and consolation, relates to the time when people are seriously ill or dying, as the following story demonstrates.

> A black SUV drove slowly down the street on a hot summer Sunday afternoon. It's tinted windows prohibited outsiders from seeing into it or recognizing the passengers. At the same time, Fr. Pedro drove out of the church's parking lot, exhausted after a morning of celebrating Masses. The two vehicles met at the end of the driveway.
>
> The SUV stopped and beeped its horn. Fr. Pedro became alarmed, for the neighborhood housed drug

dealers, often driving similar looking SUV's with tinted windows. Reluctantly, he stopped his car next to the SUV. Slowly its window opened and he saw an elderly man and woman in the front seat. The priest relaxed, figuring they were not drug dealers who might threaten him with a gun.

The man said, "Do you know where I can find a priest? Fr. Pedro dressed in civilian clothes on his way home replied, "I'm a priest, can I help you?" The anxious man in the SUV said, "Mamie, my mother, is dying and we can't find a priest to anoint her." The priest took the holy oils from his glove compartment, got out of his car, went across the street, and got into the back of the SUV. He asked the man if his mother was conscious. He said no, that she was in a coma. They went immediately to the nursing home where Mamie lived.

Entering the room, Fr. Pedro saw a woman in her nineties on a small bed with a beautiful peace radiating from her. Her immediate family stood around the bed. Initially, she made no reply, as Fr. Pedro spoke to her. So he proceeded with the rite. After the initial prayers, the priest anointed her and gave her a final blessing.

Before he left, he spoke loudly to her and said, "Mamie, I am the priest. I just anointed you. Can you hear me? If so, press gently on my hand." As he put his hand into hers, he felt a faint pressing. He continued, "Do you want to receive Holy Communion?" Her response was a stronger press. Fr. Pedro asked her son to drive him back to church to get the consecrated host. They left and in a few moments returned with the Blessed Sacrament.

As Fr. Pedro prepared to give the host to her, he

> asked her son to hold the pyx that contained it, while he dropped a small sliver of the host into a spoonful of water. This Mamie's son did with trembling hands. With family members encouraging her to keep her mouth open, the priest gave her Holy Communion.
>
> A great peace came over the room and everyone there. Fr. Pedro dropped to his knees at Mamie's bedside and held her hand. The family knelt as well. As they knelt, Fr. Pedro imagined Mary at the foot of the cross, holding the body of her recently deceased son. When the priest left the room, the family followed him. They thanked God for their faith and expressed their appreciation to Fr. Pedro. He assured them that Jesus, who died for them, would soon take their mother into heaven.
>
> On this Sunday afternoon, God smiled upon Mamie, as her family witnessed her anointing and reception of Viaticum (Communion) as she prepared to enter eternal life. It was a true celebration of the end of her earthly life and the beginning of her new life with God. Two days later, after Mamie died, Fr. Pedro received a phone call thanking him for his kindness.

Death is the fate of every human. Reflecting on Mamie's story, we remember the good thief on the cross. Like him, we are sinners. Someday, may we hear Jesus' words, spoken to the good thief, "Truly, I tell you, today you will be with me in Paradise" (Luke 23:43).

THE MAIN POINTS IN THIS CHAPTER

- Pastoral ministers can learn many lessons from the story of Jim and his garden. One of them is that endings, followed by new beginnings, always bring renewed life.
- Our attitude toward final death influences the values we associate with lesser deaths and rebirths in infancy, childhood, adolescence, adulthood, and old age. Death challenges us to question materialistic norms that distort core values associated with death and the afterlife.
- Hunger exists to serve others. Pastoral ministers can encourage parishioners to bring Christ's message of compassion into every segment of society. Even when society witnesses kindness, it cannot probe deeply into the motivation for such actions. Here, the Christian message bridges the gap.
- Mary's unwavering commitment to God reminds us to be faithful to God and our loved ones during painful times. After Pentecost, Mary's heart must have burst with joy, as she witnessed the fulfillment of Jesus' mission. Mary's response to Jesus' fate invites pastoral ministers to renew their confidence that God is with them as they move from one ministerial situation to another.
- The transition times and rites of passage surrounding endings and new beginnings provide rich opportunities for pastoral ministers to reach out and help others. They can help parents see how materialistic priorities at the beginning of life affect one's entire life.
- Sacraments assist people in their quest for a meaningful existence, and to this end, endings and new beginnings can be seen in light of the sacrament of the anointing of the sick.

As a group talk about this chapter using these questions:

- Identify three transition times or rites of passage that involved death and rebirth in your life. How and why were they important and what consequences came from them? How did the Catholic community support you?
- Reflect on significant endings during your life or the life of a loved one. To what degree did you regard them as sacred or secular events? Discuss whether or not they were occasions for probing more deeply into the mystery of God's love.
- Reflect on a significant ending in your life in light of Jim's story about the garden. What struck you from this story? What lessons can pastoral ministers learn from it?
- Discuss how modern advertising uses beginnings and endings as ways to sell their products. Cite specific instances and reflect on how such advertising influences our broader view of life and death.
- Reflect on endings in your life in light of Mary's response to Jesus' life. How does connecting our experiences with Jesus help us to keep our eyes fixed on spiritual realities during life's endings and new beginnings? Discuss how endings in Jesus' life add fresh insights to what happened to you or to someone that you know.
- How often do pastoral ministers regard endings as opportunities to bring faith and Christian concern to others? Discuss occasions of this sort that you or your parish responded to or missed.
- Discuss how the Christian virtues of love and gratitude connect with endings in your life.
- How often do pastoral ministers see that endings and new beginnings provide opportunities for faith formation?

- If you parish developed a process to help parishioners better respond to endings in their lives, what could it look like?
- How does the church's liturgical year help you appreciate the connection between faith and life's endings?
- Reflect on the story of Mamie's anointing. How is this sacrament a powerful way to connect life's ending with eternal life?

Life is a beautiful journey, marked with many transitions. These offer us the opportunity to respond in faith to God who always calls us to become more fully like Christ. In so doing, we live in the footsteps of Jesus who loves us and promises an eternal reward to those who love him.

Conclusion

As we conclude, let us ponder the beautiful words of Paul to the Colossians:

> In our prayers for you we always thank God, the Father of Our Lord Jesus Christ, for we have heard of your faith in Christ Jesus and of the love that you have for all the saints, because of the hope laid up for you in heaven…may you be prepared to endure everything with patience, while joyfully giving thanks to the Father, who has enabled you to share in the inheritance of the saints in light. He has rescued us from the power of darkness and transferred us into the kingdom of his beloved Son in whom we have redemption, the forgiveness of sins.
>
> He is the image of the invisible God, the first born of all creation, for in him all things in heaven and on earth were created…all things have been created through him and for him…and through him God is pleased to reconcile to himself all things, whether on earth or in heaven, by making peace through the blood of his cross. (1:3–5, 11–14, 16–17, 20)

These words say it all for the believer. Life includes joys and sorrows. We succeed, we fail, and we move forward. What is the purpose of good times and difficult ones? We repeat life's successes and failures in endless cycles. We take advantage of some opportunities and miss others. We are born, grow, marry, get old, and die. Life proceeds steadily toward its end. What is life's purpose? We are certain of only one event, namely, that some day we will die. And then what happens? Is there reason for it? Is death like the wind that blows nowhere or does it release us from life's inevitable sorrows and bring us the ultimate fulfillment of joy?

Jesus gives us the answers. The life transitions and rites of passage discussed in this book point to the time when we will die. Jesus tells us that this life is just the beginning of an eternal life with God, the angels, and the saints. Faith hints at what this entails, even though the afterlife is clouded in uncertainty. We believe, however, that we shall experience

> What no eye has seen, nor ear heard,
> nor the human heart conceived,
> what God has prepared for those who love him.
> (1 Corinthians 2:9)

If we believe these words, we see life differently. Then, our joys and sorrows become worthwhile. Only after we die, will we realize how really worthwhile they have been. How we live now is how we will live for all eternity. Live well!